D1083799

NORTH CAROLINA
ADVENTURE WEEKENDS

A Traveler's Guide to the Best Outdoor Getaways

NORTH CAROLINA ADVENTURE WEEKENDS

Published by Menasha Ridge Press
Distributed by Publishers Group West

First edition, first printing

Cover and interior design: Jonathan Norberg
Cover and interior photographs: Jessie Johnson and Matt Schneider, unless otherwise noted;
photos on pages 1, 2, 5, 9, 26, 32, 35, 37, 39, 42, 53, 62, 67, 68, 94, 118, 123, 153, 169, 170, 173, 185, 186, and 188 via Shutterstock.
Cartography: Scott McGrew
Typography: Monica Ahlman
Indexer: Rich Carlson

Library of Congress Cataloging-in-Publication Data
    Names: Johnson, Jessie, 1981- author. | Schneider, Matt, 1979- author.
    Title: North Carolina adventure weekends / Jessie Johnson and Matt Schneider.
    Description: First edition. | Birmingham, Alabama : Menasha Ridge Press,
      An Imprint of AdventureKEEN, [2017] | "Distributed by Publishers Group West"
      —T.p. verso. | Includes index.
    Identifiers: LCCN 2017007039| ISBN 9781634040921 (paperback) |
      ISBN 9781634040938 (ebook) | 9781634042277 (hardcover)
    Subjects: LCSH: Outdoor recreation—North Carolina—Guidebooks. |
      North Carolina—Guidebooks.
    Classification: LCC GV191.42.N72 J65 2017 | DDC 796.509756—dc23
    LC record available at https://lccn.loc.gov/2017007039

Menasha Ridge Press
An imprint of AdventureKEEN
2204 First Ave. S., Suite 102
Birmingham, AL 35233
800-443-7227, fax 205-326-1012

Visit menasharidge.com for a complete listing of our books and for ordering information. Contact us at our website, at facebook.com/menasharidge, or at twitter.com/menasharidge with questions or comments. To find out more about who we are and what we're doing, visit blog.menasharidge.com.

DEDICATION

This book is dedicated to the greatest adventure dog ever, Moe.

NORTH CAROLINA
ADVENTURE WEEKENDS
A Traveler's Guide to the Best Outdoor Getaways

Jessie Johnson and Matt Schneider

MENASHA RIDGE PRESS
Your Guide to the Outdoors Since 1982
an imprint of AdventureKEEN

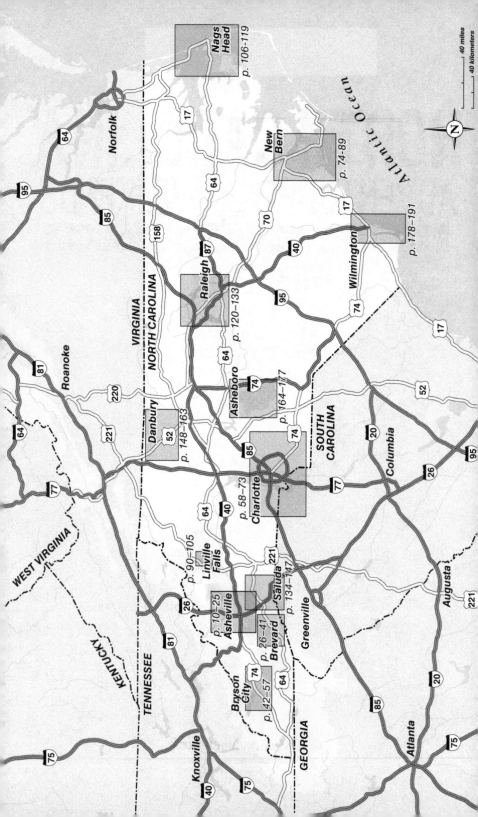

TABLE OF CONTENTS

PREFACE

■ Pilot Mountain

"Where are you guys going *this* weekend?"

We had been leaving town so many weekends, our coworkers eventually stopped asking if we were going anywhere and instead started asking where we were going. We realized we had become pretty predictable when they could answer for us: "North Carolina!"

Both of us spent a lot of time in North Carolina as children. Matt started "hiking" in the Western North Carolina mountains when he was 6 months old, and Jessie spent much of her childhood romping in the woods behind her Broadway, North Carolina, home. When we moved to northern Georgia, we were excited to live only a few hours away from North Carolina; in fact, the drive was short enough to take on a Friday night after work! Every weekend of camping in the wilds of North Carolina left us craving even more adventure in our new home away from home.

Finding the best places to get our outdoor adventure fix every weekend began consuming a lot of our time. We were always on the hunt for places to fit in as many of our favorite activities—camping, biking, hiking, paddling, climbing, and, okay, beer-tasting—as possible, with as little driving in between adventures as possible. We came to realize that we weren't alone. Most of the outdoors lovers we knew craved spending more of their free time playing outside but couldn't find the time to plan weekend trips during their busy weeks. To solve this problem, we decided to put our years of weekend adventures to good use and this book was born.

North Carolina offers adventures from the mountains to the sea. In fact, the Mountains-to-Sea Trail (MST) runs across the entire expanse of the state—and threads its way through several of our chapters. Indeed, this state is as ripe with weekend trip possibilities as your hiking clothes in mid-July. *North Carolina Adventure Weekends* puts outdoor adventure game plans at your fingertips, making it easy to pack the car and hit the road. As we researched this book, we discovered even more North Carolina locales that seemed to

■ Trail to the Narrows

White Oak River

be made for a weekend's worth of adventures. A day trip paddling down the Green River turned into two days of camping in the deep and mysterious Green River Gorge and hiking to waterfalls straight from our tent. When we camped at Carolina Beach State Park, we had planned a weekend of paddling, paddling, and oh, more paddling, but the opportunities we found to explore the terra firma on foot and bike were too irresistible to pass up. We've been asked more than a few times, "What's in the middle of North Carolina, anyway?" We respond, with no hesitation: "LOTS!" You'll find national forests, nature preserves, rivers, and even elevation changes. On a recent trip to Raleigh, we found more lakes, rivers, hiking, and mountain biking trails crisscrossing the state's capital city than we could ever conquer in just a few days.

While we can't pack the car for you, we hope this book, with its ready-to-go plans, inspires you to spend your weekends doing whatever it is that makes you happy: cooking over a glowing campfire, gripping cool rock as you scale a cliff, hiking to mountaintop vistas, carving through dirt trails on two wheels, exploring streams, marshes, and ocean, or just relaxing in a hammock as you breathe in fresh air.

This is what makes us happy. So if you see us out there, say hi!

Blue Clay Bike Park

NORTH CAROLINA ADVENTURE ACCOLADES

INTRODUCTION

Mention North Carolina, and people tend to picture the scenic **Blue Ridge Parkway** weaving its way through the western edge of the state, up and over the **Appalachian Mountains**. Or they think of the east coast, with its miles of golden sand beaches and blue-green waves crashing onto the shore. We can't blame them; the far western and eastern parts of the state are natural wonderlands. Central North Carolina is far from an outdoor adventure wasteland, however. For years, we were guilty of ignoring the middle part of the state in search of outdoor pursuits, but eventually we found several of our favorite adventure hot spots in Central North Carolina. (Here's looking at you, **Hanging Rock**.) In reality, the terrain in between the mountains and the coast is covered with national forests; state parks; paddle, hike, and bike trails; greenways; wetlands; nature preserves; and hundreds of campgrounds. Close your eyes, pick any spot on a map of the Tar Heel State, and you're likely to find some amazing adventures.

Next time you play in North Carolina's great outdoors, keep in mind that the state's topography has been a long time in the making. More than 250 million years ago, shifting plates collided and pushed Earth's crust together, forming what we now know as the Appalachian Mountains. (Back then, though, they were many thousands of feet taller!) North Carolina still boasts 43 peaks above 5,000 feet, and while people from out West might balk at calling anything under 10,000 feet a "mountain," the state's lush, tree-lined ridges and peaks offer their own elevating experience. As the mountainous west fades into the Piedmont,

1,000-plus-foot monadnocks rise from the valleys, creating hilly hikes, clifftop views, and tumbling waterfalls. Rivers that originate in Western North Carolina's mountains meander all the way across the state to the coastal plain, where they slow and spread out, providing sanctuary to wildlife and paddlers alike. As a result of the rivers' long journeys, you can find mountainous rock just a stone's throw from the coast. Speaking of which, millions of people flock to the state's idyllic beaches for a relaxing day of lounging, but there's a lot to keep them busy too: towering sand dunes, hiking trails lined with carnivorous plants, and hidden islands only accessible by boat.

If not for the foresight of Locke Craige, the state's 53rd governor, North Carolina's natural treasures might have been destroyed by the mining and timber industries. Craige lobbied for the creation of North Carolina's first state park, **Mount Mitchell State Park**, in 1915. The U.S. Forest Service stepped in with its own conservation efforts shortly thereafter, establishing **Pisgah National Forest** in 1916. Today, North Carolina is home to more than 40 state parks and recreation areas, four national forests, and 12 wilderness areas, making it a dream state for outdoor adventurers. With so many options, we don't blame you for feeling a bit overwhelmed. Relax, read, and get ready for an incredible weekend adventure!

■ Lake Fontana Spring Appalachian Trail

HOW TO USE THIS BOOK

This book introduces you to the best outdoor recreation options around the state, keeping in mind that you only have a weekend—48 hours—to explore a destination. Each location was chosen because it offers easily accessible outdoor fun and minimal travel time in between activities. Most adventures are less than half an hour away from our top pick campground, and many are right outside your tent door! Each chapter serves as a comprehensive guide for a weekend of outdoor activities, with lodging recommendations, activity descriptions, outfitters, contact information, directions, and an area map.

Whether you just bought your first pair of hiking boots or you've been hitting the trail for decades, each chapter has enough adventure options for beginners and experts alike to fill an entire weekend. Actually, there's more adventure in each chapter than any human could tackle in 48 hours, so you can piece together a weekend itinerary based on your skill level and favorite activities. And, of course, nothing's stopping you from making a 2nd, 3rd, or 15th trip to your favorite destinations! You'll find plenty of material in each chapter to keep you busy. Area maps of each destination and detailed directions will help you get the lay of the land and maximize your time outside.

LODGING 🔺

In each chapter, we recommend a "top pick" campground based on amenities, cleanliness, privacy, spaciousness, seasonal dates, and most importantly, proximity to recreational opportunities. While we love setting up our tent in a big site with scenic views, what we appreciate most on a time-crunched weekend trip is being close to all the fun things we want to do. Campgrounds that offered trails, paddling, or other recreational opportunities right from our site made it to the top of the list. In most cases, we also suggest a backup campground. Sometimes, you might even prefer the backup because of its location or the type of camping it offers (primitive vs. established, for example). If you're camping at a state park, keep in mind that most of North Carolina's state parks lock their gates and you can't enter or leave after closing time. Some campgrounds allow all their sites to be reserved, while others keep sites available on a first-come, first-served basis. In case your idea of an awesome weekend doesn't involve curling up in a tent, we also recommend a hotel or cabin—or, in one case, a grown-up version of a tree house—that we've found to be especially adventurer-friendly.

■ U.S. National Whitewater Center

BIKING 🚲

You'll find places to explore on two wheels almost everywhere in North Carolina, and each chapter directs you to the best road/ mountain biking in the area it focuses on. Some "road" bike routes actually follow the state's many miles of greenways: protected paths just for pedestrians and cyclists that often run alongside rivers and through wetlands. Other road rides are just what the name implies, as cyclists will share road space with other vehicles. When appropriate, cue sheets—easy to follow, turn-by-turn directions—are included in the road biking descriptions. Our recommended mountain bike rides take you on wide gravel roads (doubletrack) and narrow dirt, rock, and root trails (singletrack). And no, mountain biking doesn't always have to happen in the mountains! In this book, *mountain biking* refers to all off-road biking.

■ Bradley Falls creek crossing

HIKING

If you can walk, you can hike. However, not every hike is suitable for all adventurers. Keep in mind that a mile in the backcountry can feel like much more than a mile of walking around your neighborhood. Experienced hikers with certain expectations of what a hike is should know that the recommended routes don't always involve hoofing it up the side of a mountain. Coastal North Carolina is home to some beautiful trails, but they tend to be flat, sandy, and more exposed than mountain hikes. We provide general information about each recommended trail, including distance, estimated time (based on a person of average physical fitness), route-finding tips, and hike highlights. You'll also find directions to the trailhead and other pertinent information, such as gate closing times.

PADDLING

Grab that canoe, kayak, or stand-up paddleboard (SUP)! North Carolina is covered in paddle-friendly waters. You'll find some of the world's best and wildest whitewater (fast-moving water with rapids of various degrees of difficulty), but there's no shortage of family-friendly floats too. Each paddling site description in the book includes put-in and takeout information (where to start and end your paddle)

■ Falls Reservoir in the Uwharrie National Forest

and the run's difficulty rating, from Class I (small ripples) to Class V+ (violent and dangerous rapids). We also describe flatwater paddling opportunities on many of North Carolina's scenic lakes. Many of our suggested paddle trips are on horsepower-restricted or motor-free lakes and rivers, allowing you to enjoy nature without the hum of a powerboat nearby. You don't have to own a boat or have paddling experience to enjoy many of North Carolina's waterways. We recommend outfitters who rent boats, SUPs, and paddling gear and provide guide services and instruction, in case you're looking to advance your skills.

CLIMBING

Many of North Carolina's climbing routes are multi-pitch, traditional (trad) routes that require extensive experience and lots of gear. In addition to these routes, we also include the best sport and top-rope climbing areas in the state, so even novice climbers can get in on the action and enjoy a day on the rocks. We provide clear directions on how to access climbing areas and descriptions of the types of climbing you'll find there. In each chapter, you'll find route suggestions—named, predetermined paths up a specific area of rock—with their difficulty ratings. We also highlight bouldering opportunities. Bouldering is climbing done close to ground without the use of rope or harnesses, but with a thick crash pad and reliable spotters. We provide contact information for several experienced and reputable guide companies, and highly recommend that new and veteran climbers alike take advantage of their expertise and local knowledge.

■ Climbing Pilot Mountain

OTHER ADVENTURES

North Carolina's adventures aren't limited to hiking, biking, climbing, and paddling. Zipline and aerial challenge courses are proliferating throughout North Carolina, and we've highlighted ones that provide a safe, professional, and unique experience. You'll also find information on surfing, hang gliding, scuba diving, and natural watersliding.

■ Sliding Rock

MAPS

Many sites make their maps available online and at the destination. When we couldn't locate a good free map, we suggested maps that would be useful to purchase, especially if you like to get off the beaten path.

RAINY DAY

With the right gear—a water-shedding rain jacket and rain pants, a sturdy tarp or canopy, and lots of towels—adventures don't have to stop in the rain. However, seeking shelter during storms, torrential downpours, and wet, chilly weather is a smart move. Our rainy day suggestions, which range from IMAX theaters to nature museums to North Carolina historical sites, are your best bets for learning more about North Carolina's cultural and natural history while staying protected from the elements.

FOOD AND DRINK

Campsite cooking is its own adventure, but it's also fun to check out the local food scene. Whenever possible, we suggest restaurants and breweries that are local favorites, don't require you to shower beforehand, and offer a unique and affordable experience. We also prioritized dog and kid-friendly businesses. Luckily, North Carolina breweries tend to be pretty accommodating of your whole family—both tot-size and four-legged members.

GEAR AND RESUPPLY

Don't worry: everyone forgets something on a weekend adventure! For items you can't live without, we provided the locations of the closest grocery and convenience stores, gas stations, and outdoor gear outfitters. Of course, your ability to resupply will vary by destination. If you forget your tent, you'll be in much better shape if you're camping near a city center than a remote national forest. To help out outdoor gear junkies, we'll occasionally point you in the direction of local outfitters that might not be the most convenient but offer outstanding selection and service.

FAMILY FRIENDLY

You'll find family-friendly designations at the top of many activity descriptions. These options tend to be shorter, safe for kids (as long as you take proper precautions), and often have a bailout opportunity. Just because an activity isn't labeled family friendly, though, doesn't necessarily mean you have to rule it out on a trip with the kids. You know your family best, so use your judgment and ask questions. Rangers, outfitters staff, and park employees can help you decide what's appropriate.

THE LEAVE NO TRACE SEVEN PRINCIPLES

Leave No Trace™
Center for Outdoor Ethics | LNT.org

The Leave No Trace Center for Outdoor Ethics, an educational nonprofit organization whose mission is to protect the outdoors by teaching people to enjoy it responsibly, endorses seven simple guidelines that help to ensure your favorite natural places are preserved for future generations. Anyone who enjoys and cares about the outdoors—including you!—would be wise to take heed of these principles.

- **Plan Ahead and Prepare.** Doing your homework not only helps you have a safe and enjoyable outdoor experience, it also allows you to recreate in a sustainable way. Check relevant websites (included in each chapter) before you go for up-to-date information, such as fire bans, trail closures, limits on the number of people/cars/tents in a campsite, and so on. Also, making sure you have enough trash bags for litter, your own garbage, and pet waste will make a big difference.

- **Travel and Camp on Durable Surfaces.** Just building trails impacts the land. To avoid further damage, stay on established trails, hike in the middle of the trail (don't worry about puddles; your feet will dry out), and avoid cut-throughs. Keep tents, camping gear, and your vehicle in established campsite boundaries.

- **Dispose of Waste Properly.** When nature calls in the backcountry, dig a cathole 6–8 inches deep and at least 200 feet away from water sources. (Do we need to explain why?) Disguise the hole when you're done with your duty. Bury your toilet paper or pack it out in a sealed bag. When out paddling, seek opportunities to do your business on dry land, but when you're away from land for long periods of time, pack some human waste disposal bags. These smell- and leak-proof bags, readily available in outdoors stores and online, include a powder that helps to render your waste inert and can be thrown away upon your return to land.

- **Leave What You Find.** That rock, flower, or fossil was a great find, right? Leave it so others get the thrill of discovering it, just like you did. Take a picture instead and you can share your find with the world when you return to civilization and Wi-Fi. Also, leave things as you found them: don't pound nails into trees, make new campfire rings, or crush vegetation with your tent. Camping areas that become overused and "camped out" often become closed to camping.

- **Minimize Campfire Impacts.** We get it. Campfires are fun, they keep you warm, and you can make a mean s'more over an open flame. If you need a fire, use an established fire ring, and keep the fire small and contained. Big fires only burn food and clothes, anyway! To prevent pest infestations, don't bring firewood across state lines. The hemlock woolly adelgid, southern pine beetle, and emerald ash borer can hide in firewood, and these pests have already killed thousands of trees throughout North Carolina. When collecting firewood, think of it as a 4-D experience: only collect wood that is dead, down, distant (a good distance away from your camp), and dinky (smaller than your forearm).

- **Respect Wildlife.** Be considerate of wildlife in their habitat by keeping a safe distance (no selfies!), staying quiet, and never feeding them. Fed animals become nuisance animals, and nuisance animals often have to be relocated or euthanized. Food and anything else with a strong scent should be locked up in your car at night.

- **Be Considerate of Other Visitors.** Some of the best destinations get busy on weekends, but having company doesn't have to detract from your experience. Talk quietly, use headphones if you're listening to music, and keep your dog on a leash. Some trails are open to hikers, bikers, and equestrians, and communication is vital on these multiuse paths. (In preparation, practice your most polite "rider back!" call.) Cyclists yield to hikers and everyone yields to horses.

© 1999 by the Leave No Trace Center for Outdoor Ethics: LNT.org

STAYING SAFE

Many outdoor activities aren't inherently dangerous, no matter what your mom says. That said, it's important to take the proper precautions before heading out for a fun weekend. One easy way to prepare is to make sure you have the 10 Outdoor Essentials, a list of items to always have on hand when you hit the great outdoors. Note that the Boy Scouts of America created this list; if you haven't heard, they're especially known for their preparedness.

What isn't included on this list is knowledge. A map and compass won't do you much good if you don't know how to read them, and fire starters don't make the fire for you! State parks, universities, and outdoor stores, such as REI, offer free and low-cost outdoor skills classes.

10 OUTDOOR ESSENTIALS

- Extra clothing
- First aid kit
- Flashlight, headlamp, or penlight
- Map and compass
- Matches and lighters/fire starter
- Pocketknife or multitool
- Raingear
- Sun protection
- Trail food
- Water

Is it the weekend yet?

Linville Gorge rim

Bent Creek Experimental Forest is a haven for mountain bikers.

ASHEVILLE

Asheville . . . in a weekend? Yes, it can be done if you plan ahead. But you might as well bookmark this chapter because you'll definitely be coming back for more! We've carefully curated the perfect pocket of Asheville's outdoor adventures so that you can maximize your weekend playtime. Get ready to enjoy majestic views from 5,000-plus feet on Mount Pisgah, mountain bike and hike straight from your campsite in the Bent Creek Experimental Forest, paddle Class I–II rapids past Gilded Age history, and soar through treetop canopies at 65 miles per hour.

Areas included: Lake Powhatan Recreation Area, Bent Creek Experimental Forest, Pisgah National Forest, North Mills River Recreation Area, Blue Ridge Parkway, North Carolina Arboretum, local parks

Adventures: Camping, mountain and road biking, hiking, trail running, whitewater paddling, ziplining, aerial park, indoor climbing

ASHEVILLE

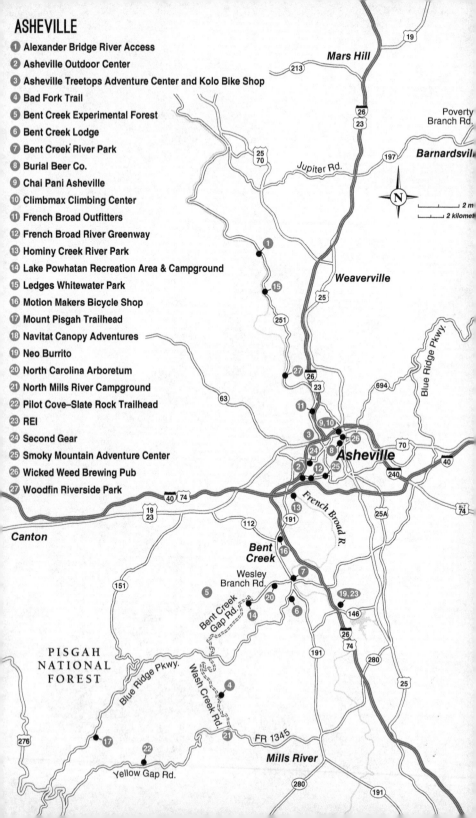

1. Alexander Bridge River Access
2. Asheville Outdoor Center
3. Asheville Treetops Adventure Center and Kolo Bike Shop
4. Bad Fork Trail
5. Bent Creek Experimental Forest
6. Bent Creek Lodge
7. Bent Creek River Park
8. Burial Beer Co.
9. Chai Pani Asheville
10. Climbmax Climbing Center
11. French Broad Outfitters
12. French Broad River Greenway
13. Hominy Creek River Park
14. Lake Powhatan Recreation Area & Campground
15. Ledges Whitewater Park
16. Motion Makers Bicycle Shop
17. Mount Pisgah Trailhead
18. Navitat Canopy Adventures
19. Neo Burrito
20. North Carolina Arboretum
21. North Mills River Campground
22. Pilot Cove–Slate Rock Trailhead
23. REI
24. Second Gear
25. Smoky Mountain Adventure Center
26. Wicked Weed Brewing Pub
27. Woodfin Riverside Park

LODGING ⛺

TOP PICK

LAKE POWHATAN CAMPGROUND (CRADLE OF FORESTRY IN AMERICA)
*375 Wesley Branch Road, Asheville; 828-670-5627; cfaia.org/lake-powhatan
-recreation-area-campgrounds-in-north-carolina. $22/night (cash or check
only), open March–November, 97 sites, reservations accepted for some sites,
picnic table, fire ring, tent pad, lantern pole, flush toilets, hot showers, some
sites share central water, some sites with water and electric (additional fee),
firewood and ice available for purchase, swimming beach*

Lake Powhatan (pronounced "Poe-uh-tun") is a popular place. If you haven't
reserved a site in advance (reservations are recommended, as the campground
often fills up), you'll be assigned a site at the camp office upon arrival. Sites on
the outside of the Hardtimes Loop back up to the woods and offer more privacy
than sites on the inside of the loop. Entering the Big John Loop, you might
be tempted to turn around at the sight of electrical hookups and big RVs, but
persevere—around the back of the loop, sites 6–18 are spacious, wooded, and
a world away from the hum of climate control. If site 27 or any surrounding
sites in the Bent Creek Loop are available,
take them and run! You'll have tons of space
for your camp toys and lots of solitude.
Lake Powhatan is located in the Bent Creek
Experimental Forest, and you can ride or
walk to the trails from your campsite in
minutes. You'll also have the French Broad
River, North Carolina Arboretum, and Blue
Ridge Parkway within a 10–20 minute
drive, so what are you waiting for? Time to
get out there!

■ Spacious campsite at Lake Powhatan

Directions *From the south* Take I-26 west to Exit 37. Turn left at end of
ramp onto NC 146 West. In 0.5 mile, turn right onto Clayton Road and
travel 1.3 miles to junction with NC 191. Turn right onto NC 191 and travel
for 1.6 miles. Turn left onto Bent Creek Ranch Road. Stay left in 0.3 mile
on Wesley Branch Road. Travel for 2.1 miles on Wesley Branch Road.
Campground is straight ahead.

From the north, west, and east Take I-26 East to Exit 33 and turn left at
the end of the ramp onto NC 191. Travel 2 miles south on NC 191 and
turn right onto Bent Creek Ranch Road and follow directions above.

North Mills River Campground (Cradle of Forestry in America) *5289 N. Mills River Road, Horse Shoe; 828-890-3284; cfaia.org/north-mills-river-recreation-area*

■ North Mills River

-campgrounds-in-north-carolina. $22/night (cash or check only), open year-round with limited facilities in winter, 31 sites, reservations accepted for some sites, picnic table, fire ring, tent pad, flush toilets, hot showers, shared water, one site with full hookup, firewood available for purchase

This campground is located alongside the North Mills River in the Pisgah National Forest. Several popular sites sit riverside, but no matter where you put your tent you're never far away from the water in this small campground.

INDOOR LODGING

Bent Creek Lodge *10 Parkway Crescent, Arden; 828-654-9040; bentcreeknc.com. $110–$205/night, Wi-Fi, full, queen, and king beds, some rooms with whirlpools, decks/balconies with wooded views, breakfast included*

The beautiful and inviting oak-beamed living room (cut from trees on the property), unbelievably comfortable beds, and rocking chairs on the secluded back deck might tempt you to forgo your adventure weekend plans. Resist! The lodge is tucked in between the Blue Ridge Parkway and the French Broad River, and is an easy drive or bike ride to Bent Creek. Plus, you'll want to work up an appetite for those reverse chocolate chip cookies.

MOUNTAIN BIKING ◉

Bent Creek Experimental Forest, a 5,500-acre section of Pisgah National Forest, is used by the Bent Creek Institute to research sustainable forest management strategies. Even cooler, it boasts 40 miles of hike, bike, and equestrian trails. Mountain bikers of all abilities can find appealing routes at Bent Creek, although beginners might be thrown off (not literally, we hope) by some of the rock gardens, root-strewn trail surface, and steep terrain. You can hike anywhere in the forest, but not all trails are open to bikes, so pick up a free trail map at the Lake Powhatan Campground office; it has trail-use guidelines, mileage, and difficulty ratings. Most trails are well marked with colored blazes, but you will find an occasional hard-to-navigate section, so bring your trail map along for the ride.

■ Bent Creek rocks

Best of Bent Creek *14-mile loop, 2–3 hours, intermediate–advanced, creek crossings, steep ascents and descents*

To reach the trailhead, ride out of the campground and take the first left onto FS 479. Turn right onto Deer Lake Lodge Trail and stay left at the intersection of Deer Lake Road (doubletrack). Shortly after that, veer left onto Wolf Branch Trail and start climbing. Continue to stay left on Wolf Branch as it intersects the Ledford Trail on the right, and then turn left onto Ledford Branch Road, passing numerous forestry experiments. Hang a right onto Boyd Branch Road, and then turn right onto the Ingles Field Connector Trail.

A quick left onto Ingles Field Gap Trail will bring you to what's known as Five Points, where North Boundary Road intersects Little Hickory Top Trail, Ingles Field, and an unnamed fifth point to the northeast. It's a great place to snack and soak in views. Take the second trail on the left, North Boundary Road, west along the side of Little Hickory Top Mountain, and continue climbing until you reach Green's Lick Trail on the left. Turn left here, hang on tight, and prepare yourself for the best descent in Bent Creek.

This trail is rocky, twisty, and somewhat treacherous, especially when wet. There are multiple jumps and drops that can be avoided, but only if you've scrubbed enough speed to spot them. At the bottom of your descent, splash through a few small stream crossings and turn left on Sidehill Trail, which climbs steadily to join with Little Hickory Top, where you'll turn left to return to Five Points. Take a right on Ingles Field Gap Trail; when the trail meets the Ingles

■ Jessie on the trail in Bent Creek

■ Matt tackles the twisty trail at Bent Creek.

Field Gap Connector, stay left to continue on Ingles Field Gap Trail. At the intersection with Ledford Branch Road, take a quick right, followed by a left onto Wolf Branch, which points downhill this time. Retrace your tracks to the Ledford Trailhead, making sure to veer right on the Deer Lake Lodge Trail where it departs the power line access road.

Bent Creek for Beginners
5 miles, 1 hour, beginner–advanced, jumps

Advanced riders can warm up on this loop and get their "mountain bike legs" underneath them, while new riders will enjoy the relatively smooth, well-built trails as they swoop through lush mountain forests. From the campground, ride south on the Powhatan Access Road toward the lake. Before reaching the lake, look for the Pine Tree Loop Trail on the right, and start your ride here. This ride is a modified figure eight, with both loops ridden counterclockwise.

After about 0.5 mile on the Pine Tree Loop Trail, turn right onto Pine Tree Connector, then right again on the Explorer Loop. Very soon after, make a left turn to stay on Explorer. In about 0.75 mile, turn left onto FS 479H and ride past the Explorer Alternate Trail. Soon after this intersection, Explorer makes a left turn back onto singletrack for a short but somewhat steep climb to the top of the hill, where you'll find the junction with Chestnut Cove Trail (hiking only). Here's where the fun really begins. Start heading downhill, and at the junction with the Explorer Alternate Trail stay right to continue on the Explorer Loop.

The trail here is fast and open, with water bars and rollers where you can (if you choose to) get some airtime. Otherwise, stay loose and sit back! As you fly down the mountain, you'll pass

■ Stop and read the signs at Bent Creek.

Sleepy Gap Trail, a 2-mile out-and-back side trip option if you'd like to add more singletrack. Near the bottom of the hill, turn right on Pine Tree Connector, then right again onto Pine Tree Loop. You can take the Pine Tree Loop back to the Powhatan Access Road to return to the campground or turn right onto the Deerfield Loop for a little more time in the woods. If you decide on the latter, stay left on Deerfield, then rejoin the Powhatan Access Road. A left turn on the Powhatan Access Road will bring you back to the campground.

Motion Makers *878 Brevard Road, Asheville; 828-633-2227; motionmakers.com*

Full-service bike shop open seven days a week, less than 10 minutes away from the Bent Creek trails, in case you need a repair or just want to pick up some maps or gear.

Kolo Bike Park *1 Resort Dr., Asheville; 828-707-4876; kolobikepark.com*

Front- and dual-suspension mountain bikes and city bikes available for rent. Feature-filled off-road bike trails right outside the front door too.

HIKING AND TRAIL RUNNING ☺

Pilot Cove–Slate Rock Loop *5.5-mile loop, 2–3 hours, moderate, creekside hiking, small cascades*

The North Mills River Area of Pisgah National Forest is often overlooked as adventurers flock to the nearby Davidson River and Bent Creek, so if you're looking for a less-traveled adventure, we highly recommend it. Start your hike heading northeast up Pilot Cove Trail, which follows a small, clear-watered tributary of Bradley Creek; several small cascades are within sight of the trail. Eventually you'll leave the creek and head steeply uphill, passing the junction of the Pilot Cove Loop Trail on the right. The Pilot Cove Loop Trail is a good route if you need a bailout option, but we recommend continuing straight, which will take you downhill along Slate Rock Creek, with its moss-covered rocks, gently gurgling water, and—in the summer months—wildflower-lined banks. The trail parallels the creek most of the way to its convergence with Bradley Creek, along Yellow Gap Road. Turn right at the road and hike 1.5 miles back to your car.

> **Directions** From Lake Powhatan, turn right onto NC 191. In 8 miles, turn right onto NC 280, then right onto North Mills River Road. In 5 miles you'll reach the North Mills River Recreation Area and campground. From the campground, continue on Yellow Gap Road (FS 1206), passing the first Pilot Cove/Slate Rock trailhead. At 6.5 miles from the campground, arrive at the second Pilot Cove/Slate Rock trailhead, located on the right.

Bad Fork Hike/Trail Run *5-mile out-and-back or 6.2-mile loop options, moderate, stream, Blue Ridge Parkway*

Trail run along Bad Creek

Short on time but want to get your trail fix? Why not take a trail run? The trail starts mildly enough as it follows Bad Creek, but don't be fooled—within 0.5 mile, you'll do an easy rock hop across the creek and your pain cave climb begins. You only gain about 700 feet in elevation, but a good chunk of it will be in the last mile, so leave something in the tank.

For the 5-mile out-and-back option, turn around at the Blue Ridge Parkway and return the way you came.

For the 6.2-mile loop option—which will be a little easier on your quads—follow Bad Fork Creek Trail for 2 miles from the trailhead, and then turn left on Wash Creek Road (usually gated), just south of the Blue Ridge Parkway. Stay left at any questionable side trail junctions and return to your vehicle on the other side of the gate for a sweet 10K trail run. Of course, this would also make a great hike if, you know, you like taking in scenery. Springtime will surround you with mountain laurels, rhododendron blooms, fire pinks, and trillium, so slowing down isn't a bad idea.

Directions Follow directions to the North Mills River Recreation Area from Lake Powhatan in the first hike. Just past the day-use North Mills Recreation Area parking lot/ on the left, and before you enter the campground, make a right turn onto FS 5000, Wash Creek Road. This road is gated at its junction with Reservoir Road, just across from Bear Branch Horse Campground. Park here, and then travel by foot past the gate on Wash Creek Road. In 0.5 mile you'll see the sign for Bad Fork Trail on the right.

■ Mount Pisgah

MOUNT PISGAH DUATHLON (HIKE AND ROAD BIKE)

Mount Pisgah Hike *3-mile out-and-back, 1.5–2 hours, moderate–difficult, outstanding views*

Pisgah Duathlon *35-mile out-and-back road bike ride and 3-mile hike, strenuous*

Hike

Ever been in downtown Asheville and noticed a tall, pointy peak standing proudly above the mountains around it? Say hello to 5,721-foot Mount Pisgah! Only about half an hour from Lake Powhatan, the rocky, rooty, and relentlessly uphill Mount Pisgah Trail leads hikers 1.5 miles up the south ridge of its namesake. At the top, you'll have sweeping views of Asheville to the east and Cold Mountain to the northwest. The first half of the hike is moderate but the second half is very steep, with lots of sloping, slippery rocks and roots. So don't be fooled—this hike is short but demanding. Once you've reached the top of Mount Pisgah, savor the views, ignore the TV transmission tower, and head back the way you came.

Duathlon

Up for some road biking on the Blue Ridge Parkway? To make this trip a true multisport adventure, you can stash your hiking shoes in a backpack and pedal your way up (and we mean UP) the twisty and steep BRP to the trailhead, enjoying this scenic route at a slower pace. If your legs are still up for it, hike up Mount Pisgah and back, and then rip downhill on the BRP to rejoin NC 191 and return to Lake Powhatan. Of course, cycling on the Blue Ridge Parkway is pretty intense and should only be attempted by experienced cyclists. Wear high visibility clothing, layer up, and make sure your bike has working lights so you can safely navigate the numerous tunnels, including one that's over 0.25 mile.

■ View from the Blue Ridge Parkway

Directions Whether driving or pedaling, leave the Lake Powhatan Campground and turn right onto NC 191. Stay in the right lane and take the exit for the Blue Ridge Parkway. Head south on the BRP for 14 miles to the Mount Pisgah parking area on the left and head to the back of the parking lot, past the Buck Spring Gap Trailhead.

PADDLING ⊗

WHITEWATER

French Broad River, Biltmore Stretch *7-mile run, Class I–II (depending on water depth), put in at the Bent Creek River and Picnic Park, take out at the Hominy Creek River and Picnic Park*

With no major difficulties, this stretch of the French Broad River Paddle Trail is perfect for paddlers who want their first taste of some mild whitewater. The river is shallow and clear for much of this route, and if you paddle softly and carry a big, um, oar, you're likely to glimpse turtles, the occasional river otter,

■ French Broad

and waterfowl, including blue and green herons, ospreys, and egrets. As you pass through the area often referred to as the Biltmore stretch, you'll get a glimpse at one of the most well-known relics of the Gilded Age, George Vanderbilt's Biltmore Estate, the largest privately owned house in the United States.

Directions to put-in From Lake Powhatan Campground, take Wesley Branch Road for 1.5 miles, and then turn right onto NC 191 South. Bent Creek River put-in is 0.5 mile down NC 191 on the left.

Directions to takeout From Lake Powhatan Campground, follow put-in directions to NC 191. Turn left on NC 191. In 4.5 miles, turn left onto Shelburne Road. After 0.25 mile, turn left onto Hominy Creek Road. The takeout will be on your left.

■ Paddling playground at Ledges Whitewater Park

French Broad River, Whitewater Surf Stretch *6–8 miles, Class I–II (possible Class III in high flow), put in at Woodfin Riverside Park, take out at Ledges Whitewater Park or at the Alexander Bridge*

This is a more urban–industrial section of the river than the Biltmore trip; however, it has better and more consistent whitewater. You can shorten or lengthen your run, depending on how much time/energy you have. There is a dam just below the put-in at Woodfin Riverside Park that you will need to portage around on river left. You can avoid this by driving north, downriver, on NC 251 and putting in below the dam. Alternatively, you can put in at Ledges and run the last third of this stretch from Ledges to just past the Alexander Bridge.

Ledges Whitewater Park is what it sounds like, and instead of a point-to-point trip, you can simply bring your play boat here and spend a few hours surfing the holes created by a broad set of shoals that stretch from bank to bank (hence, Ledges). However, if you decide to run the entire stretch from Woodfin to the Alexander Bridge, know that there are a few spots where, during higher flows, the rapids might be considered a Class III. Competent scouting will allow boaters less inclined for that sort of adventure to easily avoid them. Finally, you'll want to scout your takeout at the Alexander Bridge. There are several spots both before and after the bridge (river right) as well as on the left bank, near the railroad tracks, where you can take out; however, some of these areas are posted as private property.

Directions to put-in From Lake Powhatan Campground, leave the campground and turn left onto NC 191, following signs for I-26 West. Take I-26 west and stay right where I-40 splits to the left. Take Exit 4A on the left to stay on Future I-26 West/US 19 North. Take Exit 25 and go left at the end of the ramp onto NC 251. In 2.5 miles, you'll arrive at Woodfin Riverside Park on the left.

Directions to takeout Follow directions to put-in. From Woodfin Riverside Park, drive north on NC 251 for 4.5 miles to Ledges Whitewater Park. The takeout at the Alexander Bridge is another 2 miles north on NC 251. Just past the Alexander Post Office, you'll see the Alexander Bridge (Fletcher Martin Road) on the left.

Asheville Outdoor Center *521 Amboy Road, Asheville; 828-232-1970; paddlewithus.com*

Canoe, kayak, SUP, tube and raft rentals, shuttle services, River Oasis Taproom serving local craft beers.

French Broad Outfitters *704 Riverside Dr., Asheville; 828-505-7371; frenchbroadoutfitters.com*

Canoe, kayak, SUP, tube and raft rentals, shuttle services, disc golf gear.

VERTICAL ADVENTURES

Asheville Treetops Adventure Center
1 Resort Dr., Asheville; 877-247-5539; ashevilletreetopsadventurepark.com

Looking for a one-stop adventure shop for the entire family? Just minutes from downtown, the Adventure Center provides a day's worth of thrills for adventurers of all ages. We like the self-guided Adventure Park, where little adventurers age 4 and above can have their own fun on the kid-friendly courses or the specially designed KidZip park.

Fun at KidZip

Navitat Canopy Adventures *242 Poverty Branch Road, Barnardsville; 855-628-4828; navitat.com*

If you're in the mood to soar from mountaintop to mountaintop 300 feet off the ground, check out Navitat's Blue Ridge Experience. Even while hitting speeds of 60-plus-miles per hour you'll have plenty of time to gawk at the scenery on some of the longest and most scenic ziplines in the area.

MAPS

North Mills River, Mount Pisgah and Bent Creek Pisgah Map Company's *Western North Carolina Trail Guide: South Pisgah Ranger District Including Bent Creek*. Available at local outdoor stores (REI, Second Gear). A complete list of retailers is available at pisgahmapcompany.com/company-information /where-to-buy-our-maps.

French Broad River Riverlink.org has both a free PDF and a waterproof French Broad River access map, available at riverlink.org/experience/river-access-maps. River Link also has a mobile app available through Google Play and Apple's iTunes Store. A very detailed map and description of the French Broad Paddle Trail is available at atfiles.org/files/pdf/French-Broad-Paddle-Trail-Ogle tree2011.pdf, and an interactive app is available from Google Play and Apple's iTunes Store.

RAINY DAY

While the closest climbing opportunities are just a little too far of a drive from Asheville for a weekend adventure, there are two great indoor climbing options in town, especially if the weather is not quite as fantastic as you'd like.

Climbmax Climbing Center *43 Wall St., Asheville; 828-252-9996; climbmaxnc.com*

Indoor/outdoor climbing and bouldering for all ages.

Smoky Mountain Adventure Center *173 Amboy Road, Asheville; 828-505-4446; smacasheville.com*

Indoor climbing gym with routes ranging in difficulty from 5.5 to 5.13, bouldering and a lead wall, auto- and staff-assisted belaying, climbing gear rental, and instruction for beginners. Kid friendly and local beer on tap.

FOOD AND DRINK

Neo Burrito *Biltmore Park Town Square, 2 Town Square Blvd., Asheville; 828-772-9568; neoburrito.com*

Great place to grab a burrito on the way to camp; look up the daily passphrase on their website and grab a $1 breakfast burrito to fuel your day's adventures. You'll find beer-battered tempeh, beets, kale, and catfish, along with more traditional burrito fixings and local beer too.

Chai Pani *22 Battery Park Ave., Downtown Asheville; 828-254-4003; chaipaniasheville.com*

Indian street food sourced from local ingredients with a Southern-hipster twist. We're fans of the mixed veggie uttapam (crepes made with rice and lentil flour)—maybe it's the house-made coconut chutney that we can't resist? If you're looking for a fun culinary culture clash (and a calorie-rich fuel up), try the Bombay chili cheese fries or okra fries.

Burial Beer Co. *40 Collier Ave., South Asheville; 828-475-2739; burialbeer.com*

We like Burial for its unassuming simplicity. It has everything you need for a perfect evening at the brewery: darn good beer and a cozy courtyard that feels like a secret hiding place from the busy (and getting busier) South Slope area. Their beer runs the gamut from clean and classic pilsners to well-balanced IPAs, with a coconut porter thrown in because, well, why not?

■ Courtyard at Burial Beer Co.

Wicked Weed Brew Pub *91 Biltmore Ave., Downtown Asheville; 828-552-3203; wickedweedbrewing.com*

Because, sometimes, you want your weekend brewery stop to feel like a party. It's always an enthusiastic scene at this popular downtown hot spot. There's a restaurant upstairs, but we like to wrangle a few seats on the dog-friendly patio below, where you're bound to meet up with other adventurers. With up to 25 beers on tap—everything from German lagers to an assortment of sour offerings from their Funkatorium taproom a few blocks away—Wicked Weed will make sure all the adventurers in your group find something that they'll love (or a lot of things; did you appoint your designated driver?).

WORTH CHECKING OUT . . .

Early Girl Eatery Farm-to-table Southern comfort food, with lots of fresh, healthy options.

Laughing Seed Vegetarian cuisine that even meat eaters will devour.

Lexington Avenue Brewery Grab a flight and enjoy people-watching from the front patio of this downtown Asheville brewpub.

GEAR AND RESUPPLY 🛒

REI *Biltmore Park Town Square, 31 Schenck Pkwy., Asheville; 828-687-0918; rei.com/stores/Asheville*

It might not have local charm, but REI is less than 15 minutes away from Lake Powhatan, has an extensive selection of outdoor gear, and is open until 9 p.m.— great news when you realize you've left the tent at home.

Second Gear *444 Haywood Road, Asheville; 828-258-0757; secondgearwnc.com*

There's no guarantee on what you'll find at this well-organized outdoor gear consignment shop, but the prices, impressive selection, and friendly staff make it worth a stop.

Looking Glass Falls

BREVARD

Even if you've never been to this part of North Carolina, you've probably seen it. *The Hunger Games* movies and *The Last of the Mohicans* were filmed in Pisgah National Forest. Given the network of beautiful hiking trails, waterfalls, gnar-filled singletrack, scenic rivers, and granite cliffs, you could easily spend a week within a 10-mile radius of here and not get bored. But since you're just out for the weekend, we've distilled the best of the best for your adventuring enjoyment.

Areas included: Davidson River, DuPont State Forest, French Broad River, Looking Glass Rock, Pisgah Astronomical Research Institute, Pisgah National Forest

Adventures: Camping, mountain and road biking, climbing, whitewater paddling

BREVARD

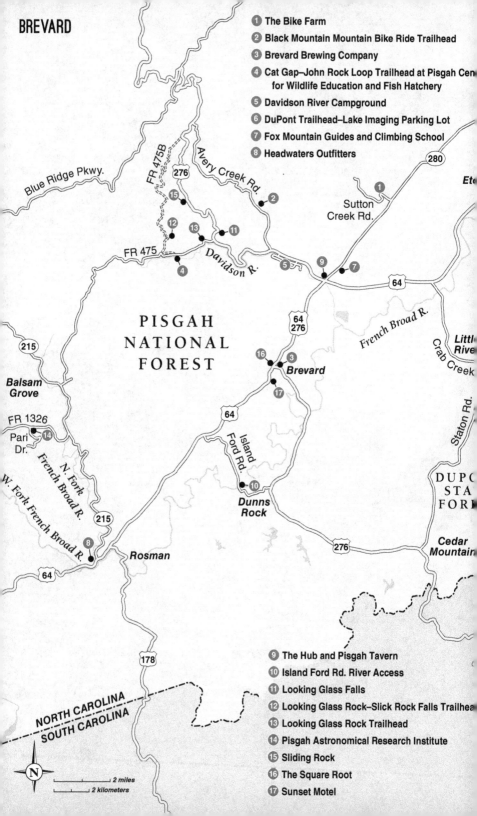

1. The Bike Farm
2. Black Mountain Mountain Bike Ride Trailhead
3. Brevard Brewing Company
4. Cat Gap–John Rock Loop Trailhead at Pisgah Cen- for Wildlife Education and Fish Hatchery
5. Davidson River Campground
6. DuPont Trailhead–Lake Imaging Parking Lot
7. Fox Mountain Guides and Climbing School
8. Headwaters Outfitters

9. The Hub and Pisgah Tavern
10. Island Ford Rd. River Access
11. Looking Glass Falls
12. Looking Glass Rock–Slick Rock Falls Trailhea
13. Looking Glass Rock Trailhead
14. Pisgah Astronomical Research Institute
15. Sliding Rock
16. The Square Root
17. Sunset Motel

PISGAH NATIONAL FOREST

Blue Ridge Pkwy.

Avery Creek Rd.

Davidson R.

French Broad R.

Brevard

Balsam Grove

Pari Dr.

N. Fork French Broad R.

W. Fork French Broad R.

Rosman

Dunns Rock

Island Ford Rd.

Staton Rd.

Crab Creek

Little Rive

Cedar Mountain

DUPO STA FOR

Sutton Creek Rd.

NORTH CAROLINA
SOUTH CAROLINA

N

2 miles
2 kilometers

TOP PICK

DAVIDSON RIVER CAMPGROUND (CRADLE OF FORESTRY IN AMERICA)

1 Davidson River Cir., Pisgah Forest; 828-862-5960; cfaia.org/davidson-river
-campgrounds-in-north-carolina. $22/night, open year-round, 160 sites,
reservations accepted for some sites, picnic table, fire ring, tent pad, lantern
pole, flush toilets, hot showers, most sites share central water, some sites
have water and electric (additional fee), Wi-Fi/plug-in station in parking lot

Davidson River is a big campground, but because it's divided into eight loops, it has a smaller feel to it, allowing you to establish your own little campground "family" if you'd like. No false advertising here: the campground is situated right along the clear, trout-filled waters of the Davidson River. Lots of sites have river views and you'll fall asleep to the lullaby of gurgling water no matter where you camp in the riverside loops.

Looking for solitude? Try to snag a first-come, first-served spot in the Laurel or Poplar Loop. Tent camper bonus: generators are not allowed in the Poplar Loop. The spacious sites in these loops are situated under a thick understory of pine, oak, and rhodo-dendron trees, and many are nes-tled within the woods. You'll feel completely separated from the rest of the campground, even though it's just a stone's throw away. If you camp in the Riverbend Loop, you'll camp close to the river and a deep swimming hole, but you'll sacri-fice privacy.

■ Sites in the Laurel and Poplar Loops allow plenty of room to spread out.

You can hike or ride the North Slope Trail or hike the Art Loeb Trail from any site, and the Syca-more Flats Trail is a short ride or drive down US 276 from the campground entrance. Though its name is uninspiring, the flat 1.5-mile Exercise Trail loops around the campground, following the Davidson River. This trail makes a great smooth-ish trail run and is especially beautiful as the setting sun reflects on the water—the perfect end to a day of awesome Pisgah adventure.

Directions From Brevard, head northeast on US 64 East/South Broad St. Turn left onto US 276 North. The campground is 1.3 miles on the left.

■ Bike Farm roadside campsite: simple and sweet

■ Cabin tents at The Bike Farm

BACKUP BASE CAMP

The Bike Farm (private) *160 Sutton Creek Road, Pisgah Forest; 828-577-3673; bikefarmpisgah.com*

Accommodations range from roadside camping with picnic tables and fire rings to deluxe canvas cabin-tents with porches, two queen beds, and two single beds. Rates are $20–$100/night. The Bike Farm also offers a well-regarded guiding service for Pisgah area mountain biking.

INDOOR LODGING

Sunset Motel *523 Broad St., Brevard; 828-884-9106; thesunsetmotel.com. $65–$99/night, Wi-Fi, cable, fridge, microwave, coffeemaker, queen and king beds*

Need an indoor base camp for your Pisgah-venture? As the motel's website advertises, you can adventure "retro-style" in this renovated 1950s roadside motel located between Pisgah National Forest and downtown Brevard. Dog-friendly rooms are available.

MOUNTAIN BIKING ⊘

Pisgah Black Mountain Rundown *11-mile loop, 3–4 hours, advanced, technical ascents and descents, creek, natural features*

Ready for some classic (that is, difficult, strenuous, and satisfying) Pisgah gnar? At the end of the parking lot, head past the gate onto FS 5058 (Clawhammer Road). Follow Clawhammer Road for 1 mile until its intersection with FS 5099/Maxwell Cove Road. Turn right onto FS 5099 and continue to climb. (Did we mention this is uphill?)

Maxwell Cove continues to wind its way north and east, narrowing from doubletrack to roomy singletrack. Reach the intersection with Black Mountain Trail at Presley Gap just past

the signed intersection with the Presley Cove Trail (foot travel only). Turn right onto Black Mountain Trail and grunt (or push) your way up and over a short climb to the top of Hickory Knob. Catch your breath at the top and lower your saddle.

For the next 1.5 miles, you'll drop steeply over roots, rocks, and ledges. No shame in a little hike-a-bike! Once you arrive at the junction of Black Mountain Trail and Thrift Cove Trail, turn right to stay on Black Mountain, an easier downhill trail section. Turn left to rejoin Thrift Cove, and then turn right onto Grassy Road. At the Sycamore Cove Trail, turn right and roll downhill. Stay left on Sycamore Cove until you come out onto US 276. Turn right and pedal 0.25 mile to Davidson River Campground.

Directions From Davidson River Campground, turn left onto US 276 and pedal 0.8 mile. Turn right onto Avery Creek Road. Follow Avery Creek Road approximately 2 miles to the horse stable parking area.

Pisgah for Mortals *9-mile loop, 2 hours, intermediate-advanced, river views, creek crossings, relatively mild Pisgah riding*

If you're not up for steep roots, rocks, and ledges, well, they're unavoidable in Pisgah. This ride, however, is less intimidating than others in the area. It's got plenty of ups and downs, but the roots and rocks are tamer than those on the Black Mountain ride. Start at the North Slope Trail parking area, located inside of Davidson River Campground.

■ Pisgah MTB

Head up North Slope (open October 15–April 15 for bikes) and stay to the right, as this trail is best ridden counterclockwise. The trail weaves along the hilly south side of the campground, eventually turning left alongside the Davidson River, then climbing sharply to the junction of the North Slope Connector Trail (foot travel only). Stay left and enjoy the undulating trail as it makes its way back toward the trailhead, finally dropping steeply back to the campground.

From there, ride out of the campground to US 276 and go straight across the road to FS 5061/Thrift Cove Road. Stay right on Thrift Cove at the junction with the Black Mountain Trail, climbing until the trail narrows and starts heading downhill. Stay left at the upper junction with Black Mountain Trail, and then turn left again to start climbing Thrift Cove once more. Turn right onto Grassy Road. At the junction with Sycamore Cove Trail, stay left and continue uphill for another mile, at which point the trail heads downhill once more, crossing several creeks and dropping you along the side of US 276. Turn right and pedal carefully back to the campground.

DuPont Flow Loop *14-mile loop, 2–3 hours, beginner–intermediate, flow, creeks, views, jumps, berms*

DuPont State Forest almost became a private enclave for the super-rich. Thanks to the efforts of The Conservation Fund, the state of North Carolina, and local conservation groups, the property—once part of the DuPont Chemical Company's X-ray film manufacturing facility—was purchased between 1995 and 2000, creating yet another shiny new jewel in Western North Carolina's crown.

This loop starts at the Lake Imaging parking lot. Head east on Lake Imaging Road. Continue past the end of Ridgeline Trail on the left, and then turn left onto Jim Branch Trail. The 1.5-mile climb up Jim Branch rewards you with some fast rollers at the top of the hill. At the intersection with the Isaac Heath Trail, turn right, and ride Isaac Heath to its junction with the Locust Trail. Continue straight onto Locust. Within 0.5 mile, Locust will drop you back onto Lake Imaging Road. Take a right, then an immediate left onto the mile-long Hilltop Trail.

Hilltop is a swoopy, fun ride that keeps the speed going all the way to its junction with Grassy Creek Falls Trail. Take a left and then an immediate right onto Lake Imaging Road. Turn right again at the next intersection onto Buck Forest Road. Soon after crossing the bridge, turn left onto the unsigned Chestnut Oak Road, which begins with a steep climb. Watch for Oak Tree Trail on the left, within 0.25 mile. (For some reason, the sign for Oak Tree Trail is on the right.) Oak Tree is one of the most technical trails on this loop, with steep, rocky climbs that give riders a taste of the slickrock that's exposed throughout the forest. But the trail is only 0.5 mile, so it's no sufferfest.

Grassy Creek Falls

At the end of Oak Tree, turn left onto Joanna Road and enjoy the break from steep climbs and technical riding. Continue 0.75 mile past Table Rock Trail to the junction with Twin Oaks Trail. Turn right on Twin Oaks and enjoy this lesser-ridden 1-mile downhill to the junction with Briery Fork Trail. Turn right onto Briery Fork (1.3 miles) and continue your downhill cruise. Ford Briery Fork, pass the right-hand junction with Turkey Knob, and cross Briery Fork again before climbing back to the junction with Joanna Road and Grassy Creek Trail. Cross Joanna Road to continue downhill on Grassy Creek Trail (1 mile), and then cross Grassy Creek and turn right onto Sandy Trail. You'll immediately come to a junction with Wintergreen Falls Trail. Turn right to take a side trip to Wintergreen Falls (foot travel only), then turn around and follow Wintergreen Falls Trail uphill (a left turn from the Sandy/Wintergreen junction) to Tarkiln Branch Road. Turn right onto Tarkiln Branch and follow it for just under a mile, passing several logging roads on the right to where the trail splits. Veer right and head past a gate onto Sky Valley Road. Turn left onto Sky Valley then immediately right onto the sometimes-signed Shoal Creek

■ View from Davidson River campsite

Trail for a straight-shot 1.2 miles downhill to rejoin Sky Valley Road. Turn right onto Sky Valley, and then take the first left onto the 0.5-mile Rifle Trail. Take Rifle uphill to the junction with Guion Trail. Turn left on Guion and left again at Hickory Mountain Road. Take the next right onto White Pine Trail. Just as you begin to gain speed, turn right again onto 1.1-mile Hooker Creek Trail.

Hooker Creek has lots of fast rollers, so be careful to keep the rubber side down. Eventually you begin climbing again to Ridgeline Trail. Turn left onto Ridgeline and hold on—this is the most famous 1.5 miles at DuPont for good reason: flow. You'll be able to maintain your speed around bermed turns, over groomed jumps, and over (or around) trail features such as log rides and skinnies. Pop out on Lake Imaging Road, and then turn right to return to your car.

Directions From Davidson River Campground, turn right onto US 276 and go straight 4.9 miles. In Penrose, turn right onto Crab Creek Road and follow it 4.3 miles. Turn right at DuPont Road (there are signs for DuPont State Forest). In 2.6 miles, the Lake Imaging parking area is on your left.

Estatoe Trail and Brevard Bike Path *10-mile out-and-back, 1–2 hours, easy, protected bike path, river views, downtown Brevard*

This 5-mile, one-way crushed gravel and asphalt trail begins in the Art Loeb Trail parking lot, just before the bridge at the entrance to Davidson River Campground. Jump on the trail at the end of the parking lot (heading around the gate) and follow the Davidson River into Brevard. Once you reach Lowe's, proceed on the Brevard Bike Path, which you can take almost all the way to downtown Brevard. Hit up town for a quick refuel—the kids (or the kid in you) won't complain too much about the trip back after a milkshake at Rocky's Grill and Soda Shop, especially if you throw in a trip to O.P. Taylor's Toy Shop. Just don't forget your wallet and a backpack or two for your loot.

For bike shop information, see The Hub on page 40.

HIKING ☁

Looking Glass Rock *6.4-mile out-and-back, 3 hours, moderate–difficult, streamside hiking, peak views*

Looking Glass Trail

This popular hike takes you to the top of Looking Glass Rock, where you'll soak in majestic views. The Looking Glass Rock Trail starts from the parking lot with a moderate climb along a small, pretty stream. If there's been a recent rain, you'll catch glimpses of some cascades as you move up the mountain. The forest begins to open up and your legs will be thanking the trail builders who created the numerous switchbacks on this trail, keeping the climb quite manageable. At mile 2.3, you'll reach the Transylvania County Rescue Squad's helipad, which is a nice, flat spot to sit and take a pit stop, if needed. After this point, the trail climbs more steeply and is quite eroded in some sections. Avoid contributing to future trail degradation by hiking in the center of the trail whenever possible. Around mile 3, your climb temporarily plateaus on a chunk of flat rock surrounded by trees. Don't panic—your views are still coming. Push through the rhododendron tunnel for the last 0.5 mile and be rewarded by 180-degree views of the Pisgah Ridge, Black Balsam Mountain, Shining Rock, Mt. Pisgah, and the Blue Ridge Parkway. Return the way you came, enjoying gravity's natural assistance. This is a very popular hike, especially on weekends, so the earlier you get out the more solitude you'll enjoy. Rise and shine, campers!

> **Directions**   From Davidson River Campground, take US 276 for 4 miles. Turn left onto FS 475 (Davidson River Road) at the sign for the Pisgah Center for Wildlife Education and Fish Hatchery. Trailhead parking lot is 0.4 mile on the right.

Cat Gap–John Rock Loop   *4.4-, 6-, and 8.3-mile loop options, moderate–difficult, streams, some rock-hopping, waterfalls, views, shelter*

This hike offers major bang for your buck, with a variety of loop options and lots of great scenery. Start your hike on the Cat Gap Loop Trail near the kiosk, at the opposite end of the parking lot from the Wildlife Education Center. Cross the bridge over Cedar Rock Creek and enjoy the easy stroll alongside this gentle creek. As the trail rises, you'll encounter your first route choice. At mile 1.25, turn right onto John Rock Trail to hike 1.7 miles up and over John Rock. Alternately, you can continue straight on the Cat Gap Loop.

■ Cedar Rock Falls

If you choose John Rock (a 6-mile round-trip), tell your legs to be ready because you'll start climbing immediately. Even with switchbacks, you'll ascend almost 500 feet in 0.5 mile. Exposed outcrops lead to a broad ridgetop and side trails lead to views off of either side of John Rock. Be careful—some hikers have lost their dogs over the side of the cliff.

Either option (John Rock or Cat Gap) will bring you to the junction of Cat Gap Loop, John Rock, and Cat Gap Bypass Trails. The short bypass avoids elevation gain and reconnects with Cat Gap Loop Trail in 0.8 mile for a 4.4-mile round-trip, whereas Cat Gap continues up to its eponymous gap. Here, it meets up with the Art Loeb Trail before descending back down toward Picklemeister Fields and the junction with the Butter Gap Trail. To tackle the 8.3-mile option, when the Cat Gap Loop Trail meets the Art Loeb Trail, take Art Loeb for 2 miles around the summit of Cedar Rock Mountain, and then turn northwest toward Butter Gap and stop for a snack at the A-frame Butter Gap shelter. Continue on Art Loeb approximately 0.6 mile to its junction with Butter Gap Trail. Follow Butter Gap downhill for 3.1 miles to join the Cat Gap Loop Trail at Picklemeister Fields; pass Grogan Creek Falls on the right and the junction with Long Branch

Creek Trail on your way. Stay left on the Cat Gap Loop Trail as it descends on an old road grade past Cedar Rock Creek Falls on the right. You will eventually cross Cedar Rock Creek and its small tributaries several times before heading over a rise and dropping back down to the Fish Hatchery parking area.

Directions From Davidson River Campground, take US 276 for 4 miles. Turn left onto FS 475 (Davidson River Road) at the sign for the Pisgah Center for Wildlife Education and Fish Hatchery. Travel 1.4 miles and park in the center's lot.

PADDLING ⊗

WHITEWATER

French Broad River *10-mile run, 3–4 hours, Class I–II, put in at Headwaters Outfitters, take out at Island Ford Bridge*

■ The French Broad sits right behind the Headwaters Outfitters sign.

Our pick for a good half-day paddling trip starts just west of Brevard at Headwaters Outfitters. As the name suggests, these are the true headwaters of the mighty French Broad River. Put in your boat just downstream of the confluence of the North and West forks of the Broad. There is a small Class II rapid just past the put-in, but if you'd prefer to avoid it, put in at Champion Park in Rosman, off of Old Turnpike Road. The 10-mile paddle from the Outfitters to the Island Ford Bridge takeout will take most paddlers about 3–4 hours, passing very little in the way of development and affording beautiful views of the bucolic valley. Leave a car at Island Ford Bridge or schedule a shuttle from Headwaters Outfitters for around $30.

Directions to put-in From Davidson River Campground, turn right onto US 276 South. After 1.2 miles, turn right onto US 276/64 West and continue 2.9 miles. Turn right onto N. Caldwell St., and after 1.1 miles turn right onto US 64 West. Drive 8.3 miles, and then turn right onto NC 215 North. Headwaters Outfitters is on the left.

Directions to takeout From Headwaters Outfitters, turn left onto US 64 East. Continue 5.5 miles, and then turn right onto Island Ford Road. Boat launch is 2 miles on the left.

Headwaters Outfitters *25 Parkway Road, Rosman; 828-877-3106; headwatersoutfitters.com*

Canoe and kayak rentals for 3-, 4-, and 7-hour trips. Shuttles, tubing, and ziplining too.

CLIMBING

Looking Glass Rock *Trad climbing; 5.8–5.13; best in fall, winter, and spring; 0.5- to 1-mile hike to cliffs*

Looking Glass Rock is an iconic feature of this area, and you can catch views of it from many of the surrounding ridges. It's also a classic traditional ("trad") climbing spot with many hundreds of feet of exposed granite and multi-pitch climbs. The Nose is one of the most classic routes, accessible to most climbers with trad-climbing expertise. There are countless other routes, both official and otherwise, but just about all of them require passive protection, anchors, and multiple ropes. If a day on slab and crack granite is your idea of a good time, head to Looking Glass. Slick Rock Falls Trail is a moderate 1-mile hike past the falls to the bottom of the south face of Looking Glass. To access the west and north faces, continue up FS 475B 1.5 miles to either the Sunwall Trail (0.5 mile) or drive 0.2 mile farther to the North Face Trail (0.8 mile). Our recommendation for climbers who know their stuff—those who own and are familiar with tricams, nuts, runners, and multi-pitch lead climbing—is to check out *Selected Climbs in North Carolina* by Yon Lambert and Harrison Shull. Another good online resource is mountainproject.com/v/looking-glass-rock/105873294. For those of you who have climbing experience but not the courage to tackle Eastern granite on your own, check out Fox Mountain Guides, located just up the road.

Looking Glass Rock

Directions From Davidson River Campground, take US 276 for 4 miles. Turn left onto FS 475 (Davidson River Road) at the sign for the Pisgah Center for Wildlife Education and Fish Hatchery. Drive about 0.75 mile and turn right onto gravel FS 475B. The first cliff access is from the Slick Rock Falls Trailhead on the right, approximately 0.7 mile up FS 475B.

Fox Mountain Guides *3228 Asheville Hwy., Pisgah Forest; 888-284-8433; foxmountainguides.com*

Instruction and guiding for all levels of climbers, including beginners.

WATER ADVENTURES

Looking Glass Falls

One of the area's most iconic landmarks, this impressive 60-foot waterfall is located just past the intersection of US 276 and FS 475, on the right. You can park roadside or take the steps down for a closer view of these powerful falls. On a hot day (or any day, if you're feeling brave), you can carefully venture out onto the rocks and dip into the pool below the falls at lower flow times. We like to brew early morning coffee in camp, and then head to these falls before they get busy.

Looking Glass Falls

■ Sliding Rock

Sliding Rock *Open May–Sept. (check www.fs.usda.gov for seasonal dates), life-guards on duty and bathrooms open 10 a.m.–6 p.m., $2 fee*

Want to feel like a kid again, ice down aching muscles, and get a natural post-adventure bath? Don't miss Sliding Rock, a 60-foot rock waterslide that launches you into a pool of cold (50°F–60°F) mountain water at its bottom. Be prepared to brave the crowds—this is a popular spot, especially during summer camp season. And, while *natural waterslide* might not sound like a hard-core activity, water shoes and rugged shorts are recommended.

> ***Directions*** From the Pisgah National Forest entrance, take US 276 about 7.5 miles.

MAPS

Pisgah National Forest Pisgah Map Company's S*outh Pisgah Ranger District.* Available for purchase at The Hub.

DuPont State Recreational Forest Pisgah Map Company's *DuPont State Recreational Forest.* Available for purchase at The Hub.

RAINY DAY

Pisgah Astronomical Research Institute *1 Pari Dr., Rosman; 828-862-554; pari.edu*

Cloudy night skies or rainy days getting you down? PARI was built in the 1960s by NASA to track satellites and unmanned space flights. Now a nonprofit educational research center, it hosts an impressive collection of telescopes. Visitors can take a self-guided tour of its Galaxy Walk and explore all 26 meters of the first satellite used to communicate with astronauts. Admission is free.

FOOD AND DRINK 🍴

The Square Root *33 Times Arc, Brevard; 828-884-6171; squarerootrestaurant.com*

From sweet tea–brined grilled pork ribeye to adventure appetite–size salads, this is the place for a more adventurous meal experience than roasted campfire weenies. Sit outside on the cozy, covered deck and watch the world—or at least Brevard—go by. Whatever you order, their zucchini fries make a perfect side. Open for lunch and dinner; closed Tuesdays.

Brevard Brewing Company *63 E. Main St., Brevard; 828-885-2101; brevard-brewing.com*

Although this brewery only opened its doors in 2012, it has the feel of a place that's been around for much longer. With a focus on classic German lagers and American Ales—no wild and wacky brews here—their beers are fresh, crisp, and comforting after a day of adventuring. There's always a good mix of locals and visiting adventurers, you can warm up as the sun shines in the huge front windows, and kids and outside food are both welcome.

Pisgah Tavern at The Hub *11 Mama's Place, Pisgah Forest; 828-884-8670; thehubpisgah.com*

"Ride bikes. Drink beer." With its relocation in 2016 to a bigger space that includes an expanded taproom with a dizzying selection of local beers, the Pisgah Tavern has made it easier than ever to live by its motto. There's cozy seating inside, a covered deck, and plenty of outdoor space for kids to run off energy while you rehash the day's adventures.

GEAR AND RESUPPLY 🛒

From Davidson River Campground, turn right onto US 276 South and then right again onto US 276 South/US 64 West to get into Brevard, where you'll find numerous grocery stores.

The Hub and Pisgah Tavern *11 Mama's Place, Pisgah Forest; 828-884-8670; thehubpisgah.com*

Full-service bike shop, bike rentals, outdoor clothing, camping supplies, maps, guidebooks, and beer on tap in the tavern to boot. Did we mention you can hit the trails straight from their parking lot?

Davidson River

Fontana Lake

BRYSON CITY-NANTAHALA GORGE

We think this area was made especially for amazing weekend adventures. Camp at Tsali Campground and ride from your tent to the trails in under 2 minutes. After hitting the trail, take a swim or paddle in the calm, clear waters of Fontana Lake. Ready for more? Paddle the Nantahala and Tuckasegee Rivers, hike in Great Smoky Mountains National Park (GSMNP), and grab some grub riverside. Rise with the sun and you just might be able to do it all in one day!

Areas included: Nantahala National Forest, Great Smoky Mountains National Park, Tsali Recreation Area, Fontana Lake, Nantahala River, Tuckasegee River

Adventures: Camping, mountain biking, hiking, whitewater and flatwater paddling, creek exploration

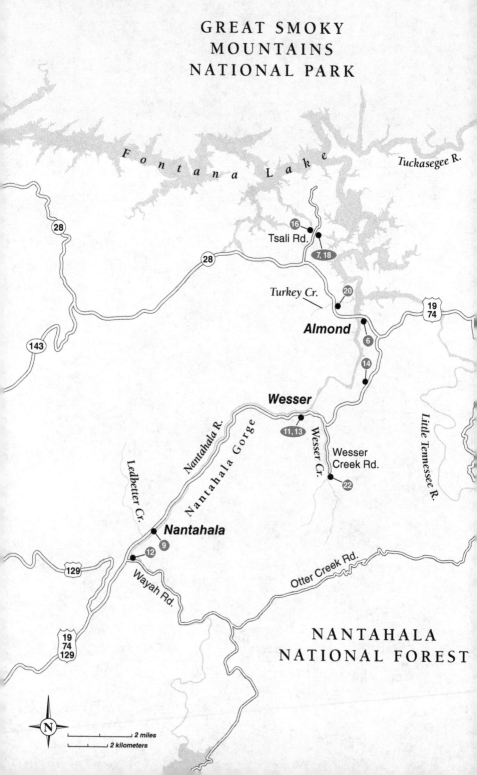

GREAT SMOKY
MOUNTAINS
NATIONAL PARK

F o n t a n a   L a k e

Tuckasegee R.

28

28

16

Tsali Rd.

7, 18

Turkey Cr.

20

19
74

Almond

6

14

Wesser

11, 13

Wesser Cr.

Wesser
Creek Rd.

Little Tennessee R.

Nantahala R.

Nantahala Gorge

Ledbetter Cr.

22

Nantahala

12   9

129

Wayah Rd.

Otter Creek Rd.

19
74
129

NANTAHALA
NATIONAL FOREST

N

2 miles

2 kilometers

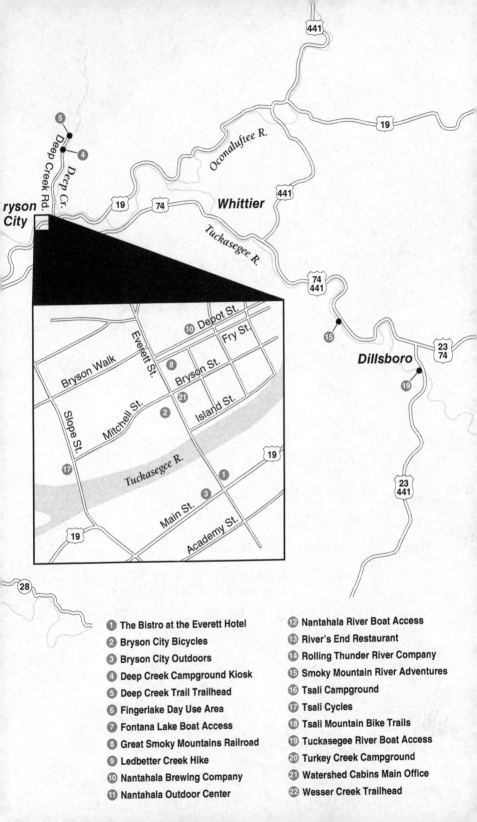

1 The Bistro at the Everett Hotel
2 Bryson City Bicycles
3 Bryson City Outdoors
4 Deep Creek Campground Kiosk
5 Deep Creek Trail Trailhead
6 Fingerlake Day Use Area
7 Fontana Lake Boat Access
8 Great Smoky Mountains Railroad
9 Ledbetter Creek Hike
10 Nantahala Brewing Company
11 Nantahala Outdoor Center
12 Nantahala River Boat Access
13 River's End Restaurant
14 Rolling Thunder River Company
15 Smoky Mountain River Adventures
16 Tsali Campground
17 Tsali Cycles
18 Tsali Mountain Bike Trails
19 Tuckasegee River Boat Access
20 Turkey Creek Campground
21 Watershed Cabins Main Office
22 Wesser Creek Trailhead

TOP PICK

TSALI CAMPGROUND *Tsali Road off NC 28, Almond; 828-479-6431; www.fs.usda .gov. $15/night, open April 1–October 31, 41 sites, first come, first served, picnic table, fire ring, lantern pole, grill, flush toilets, hot showers, central water, no electrical hookups*

Tsali (pronounced "Solly") was named after the defiant Cherokee leader who brokered a deal to allow the Native Americans, now known as the Eastern Band of the Cherokee, to remain in their ancestral territory. Its spacious, wooded campsites, best for tent campers and small RVs, are first come, first served, and often fill up on fair weather weekends. If you're heading here for a summer or early fall adventure, try to arrive early Friday afternoon, or you

■ Relaxing at Tsali Campground

might find the campground full by nightfall. Another way to snag a site on a busy weekend is to arrive on Saturday morning. We've often seen campers pack up first thing on Saturday, leaving a few sites up for grabs.

This U.S. Forest Service campground is divided into two loops, each with its own bathhouse with flush toilets and showers. Most sites are big enough to house two four-man tents, and you'll find lots of sturdy hammock-hanging trees. Our favorite sites are the ones located on the outside of either loop. These sites back up to a wooded hillside and a gurgling stream that will lull you to sleep on its way to Fontana Lake. The lake is easily accessible, either via a trail from the back of the far loop or a walk or ride down Tsali Road to the boat ramp. (We prefer the latter.)

■ Tsali sites are great for sharing.

Directions *From the east:* Take US 74 West to its merger with NC 28. Continue on US 74/NC 28 for 3.1 miles until NC 28 separates on the right. Exit right to stay on NC 28 for 3.5 miles. Just past the Swain County–Graham County line, turn right onto Tsali Campground Road. In 1.6 miles, the campground will be on the left.

From the west Take US 129 South into North Carolina. From the North Carolina line, travel 0.7 mile and turn left onto NC 28. Take NC 28 for 28.4 miles and turn left at Tsali Campground Road. In 1.6 miles, the campground will be on the left.

■ Favorite swim spot on Fontana Lake

From the north and south Take US 441 South (coming from Tennessee) or North (coming from North Carolina or Georgia) to US 74 West. Take US 74 West to NC 28 and follow directions above from the east.

BACKUP BASE CAMP

Turkey Creek Campground (private) *135 Turkey Cove Road, Almond; 828-488-8966; turkey-creek.com. $11/night/person, $4 vehicle charge, open mid-March–mid-November (call for current dates), 79 sites, reservations accepted, most sites have water and electric, picnic table, fire ring, flush toilets, hot showers, firewood and ice for sale, dump station, Wi-Fi*

Turkey Creek is located about 3 miles from the Tsali trails. Campsites are on the small side, so snag a site for each tent in your group. It's a clean, well-run campground with a swanky bathhouse and coffee and baked goods for sale on weekend mornings.

INDOOR LODGING

Watershed Cabin Rentals *Locations vary, 888-604-3075, watershedcabins.com*

Want to end (or begin) your amazing day by soaking in a hot tub? Watershed Cabins offer luxury cabin rentals throughout the greater Bryson City area. We've had the pleasure of staying in several, and all have been immaculate, comfortable, and beautiful. Rates vary.

Nantahala Outdoor Center (NOC) *13077 W. US 19, Bryson City; 828-785-4834; noc.com. Starting at $39.99 for two beds, heat and air-conditioning, shared bathrooms, showers, kitchen space, and grill*

NOC is located on the Nantahala River takeout. The Appalachian Trail runs straight through the property, and NOC has cut an intermediate-level bike trail into Flint Ridge, just behind the bunkhouses.

MOUNTAIN BIKING ⚙

While DuPont and Pisgah State Forests have become the talk of the Western North Carolina mountain biking world, the Tsali Recreation Area Trail System offers a great set of intermediate level trails that challenges beginners and keeps things interesting for veteran riders. The views are plentiful, the climbs are just long enough to get your heart rate up, and the downhills will put a silly grin on your face.

In the past few years, the Nantahala chapter of the Southern Off-Road Bicycle Association (SORBA) has taken on trail maintenance, and while you'll still find windfalls and typical lush summer overgrowth, the trails are generally in great shape. Thank you, SORBA volunteers!

If you're camping at Tsali, climb the short hill out of the campground and pay your $2 permit fee at the far end of the bike parking lot. You'll find maps, a pit toilet, and a bike wash station here.

The trail system is divided to keep mountain bikers and equestrians separated, but hikers can use the trails any time. Depending on the day, cyclists have access to either the Right and Left Loops *or* the Mouse Branch and Thompson Loops. The trail schedule changes throughout the year, so check the sign at the trailhead before riding. Trails have a recommended direction of travel, so follow the signs to reduce your chance of a collision and always be on the lookout for riders coming your way. These trails are fairly straightforward and it's difficult to get lost, as they're blazed, signed, and now include full-color trail maps at major intersections.

■ Mouse Branch Overlook

Mouse Branch Loop *8.7 miles, 1 hour, beginner–intermediate, overlook, lake views*

From the Tsali Campground, turn right onto the gravel access road for the Mouse Branch and Thompson loops. You'll immediately pass the end of Thompson on the left, and then 0.25 mile later, the end of Mouse Branch on the right. Just past the end of Mouse Branch is the trailhead for both loops.

■ Tsali Trails

You'll be traveling clockwise on Mouse Branch. Veer right onto the trail, starting with an easy downhill, followed by a steady climb. At the top, turn right to complete the last 3.5 miles of the loop or turn left to climb to the Mouse Branch Overlook Loop. The climb to the overlook is somewhat technical, but you'll be rewarded with stunning views of the Great Smoky Mountains and Fontana Lake.

Soak up the best views in Tsali, and then bomb down a switchback-laden descent that's longer and more technical than the ascent. Be sure to scrub enough speed to maneuver around several sneaky sharp turns. Cross a bridge and climb back to rejoin Mouse Branch. Turn left and retrace about a mile of previously ridden trail to the T-intersection with the overlook loop. Turn right and enjoy the brown ribbon of dirt back to the access road junction with Thompson. Take a hard left to return to camp or the parking lot, or continue ahead to ride Thompson.

Thompson Loop *7.3 miles, 1 hour, beginner–intermediate, fast and flowy, long descents, jumps, lake views*

This loop is our favorite of the Tsali set. From the three-way intersection at the end of the Mouse Branch/Thompson access road, veer left to start your fast and swoopy counterclockwise ride on Thompson. This trail is generally smooth and fast, but large roots will occasionally seem to appear out of nowhere, so watch out when it's wet. After several miles of mostly downhill cruising, you'll eventually have to pay the piper. Thompson climbs steadily for the last few miles prior to its final downhill run. At the top of a doubletrack climb at mile 6.5, turn left for one last short ascent, then hold on tight for a wildly fast downhill. You'll finish near the start of the gravel access road. Turn right and return to camp.

Right Loop *13.9 miles, 2 hours, beginner–intermediate, flowy, lake views, optional overlook, bailout options*

■ Boat launch at Fontana Lake

Start your counterclockwise Right Loop ride from the back of the mountain bike parking lot. You'll enjoy a smooth descent and flowy turns for the first several miles before eventually getting down and dirty. Along the way, you'll pass two signed "bypass" shortcuts on the left that lead to County Line Road and back to the horse parking area, located just above the bike parking lot where you started. Young or beginner riders can take the first bypass to complete a 5-mile loop of accessible singletrack and gravel road riding.

Continuing ahead, you'll grunt through several steep and technical climbs. If you're feeling adventurous, take the 2-mile Overlook Loop (not recommended for beginners) for a scenic view of Fontana Lake. Around mile 8.5, you'll arrive at the junction of the Left Loop and Left Loop Overlook Trails. Turn left for a very steep climb to the top of County Line Road, where you're rewarded with several miles of fast downhill back to the horse parking area. Here, continue down the gravel road to the campground/parking lot or turn right onto Left Loop.

Left Loop *11.9 miles, 2 hours, beginner–intermediate, creek crossings, lake views, overlook option*

From the parking lot, the Left Loop runs clockwise, starting with (appropriately) a left turn, just past the bike wash area. At 0.25 mile, ride across the horse parking lot and pop back onto the trail.

Fast and twisty, with a few sustained climbs, the Left Loop winds around lake coves, sometimes clinging perilously to the side of the mountain with a straight drop into the lake on the left. Watch out here—Matt once tumbled off the trail toward the lake. No need to worry, as he obviously lived to tell the tale and still thinks the Left Loop is worth riding!

Before you climb back up County Line Road toward the end of the loop, you'll come to the junction for the 2-mile Overlook Loop. Continue straight ahead to ride this loop, but know that it's pretty steep and technical riding.

To skip the overlook take a hard right turn at the junction. You'll arrive at the junction with Right Loop, County Line Road, and the end of the Left Loop Overlook Trail. Turn right (uphill) and follow County Line Road to the trailhead.

Deep Creek Trail (Great Smoky Mountains National Park) There's scenic and accessible gravel-road riding on the Deep Creek Trail in Great Smoky Mountains National Park, 30 minutes from Tsali. This is a great option for a good, old-fashioned family bike ride and is one of the few places in the entire park where you can ride off-road on two wheels.

Bryson City Bicycles *157 Everett St., Bryson City; 828-488-1988; brysoncitybicycles.com*

Bikes, repair, gear, friendly service and advice, and lots of affordable rental options.

Tsali Cycles *35 Slope St., Bryson City; 828-488-9010; tsalicycles.com*

Bikes, repair, rentals, weekly Tsali rides—beer and wine too!

HIKING

Reminder: No dogs are allowed on GSMNP trails. We know; it makes us sad too, but it's for the good of the park.

Indian Creek, Deep Creek, and Martin's Gap *12-mile loop, 4–6 hours, moderate, multiple waterfalls, swimming holes, ridgeline hiking*

■ Tom Branch Falls

Just minutes from downtown Bryson City lies GSMNP's Deep Creek Campground and the trailhead for the Deep Creek and Indian Creek Trails. Both of these trails are old road grades and this hike consists of mostly gentle ups and downs, with the exception of the stretch over Martin's Gap.

Start at the Deep Creek Trailhead, stopping to ogle at Tom Branch Falls on the right at 0.3 mile. Follow Deep Creek to its junction with Indian Creek Trail at 0.7 mile. Turn right onto Indian Creek Trail, where you'll find Indian Creek Falls on the left within 0.1 mile. Continue straight past three signed trail junctions. At 4.5 miles, Indian Creek Trail ends and becomes Martin's Gap Trail, which takes you up and over Sunkota Ridge to Deep Creek

Trail. At mile 6, continue straight on Martin's Gap Trail at the junction with the Sunkota Ridge Trail for 1.5 miles, and then turn left on Deep Creek Trail. Follow Deep Creek back to the trailhead for a relatively easy and incredibly scenic 12-mile loop with little elevation change.

Want just a little bit more? At the trailhead, veer right onto Juney Whank Falls Trail for a 0.6-mile out-and-back moderate hike to the 80-foot Juney Whank Falls.

Directions From Tsali Campground, turn right onto Tsali Road and then left onto NC 28 south. Continue 3.5 miles, then turn left onto US 19 North/US 74 East and drive 5.2 miles. Turn left to continue on US 74 East. After 3 miles, take Exit 67 for Bryson City and turn left onto Spring St. After 0.7 mile turn right onto Main St. and then left onto Everett St. Quickly turn right onto Island St., which then turns left and becomes Ramseur St. Turn right onto Deep Creek Road and then right again to stay on Deep Creek Road. Turn left onto East Deep Creek Road and follow signs to the campground.

Deep Creek Jaunt *4.6-mile loop, 2–3 hours, moderate, waterfalls, creekside hiking*

This hike is a shorter version of the first one. You won't get as much time in the deep backcountry (read: away from the tube-toting masses), but you'll still get your waterfall fix and the crowds will thin once you hit Indian Creek Trail. Follow the trailhead directions in the first hike. Start on the Deep Creek Trail and then turn right onto Indian Creek Trail. At mile 1.5, turn left onto the Deep Creek Loop Trail, which climbs steadily up to the junction with the Sunkota Ridge Trail, on the right, and then descends back down the hill to the junction with Deep Creek Trail at mile 2.8. Turn left onto Deep Creek Trail to return to the trailhead.

■ Tubing down Deep Creek

Wesser Creek and Appalachian Trail to Wesser Bald *9-mile out-and-back, 4–6 hours, strenuous, views, observation tower*

Wesser Creek Trail used to be part of the Appalachian Trail, before the AT was rerouted down the side of the ridge, where it crosses the Nantahala River at NOC. However, this stretch of trail is still the most direct route from valley to summit, and it's hiked enough to keep the trail clear.

Head south along Wesser Creek Trail 4 miles to the junction with the AT. Turn left onto the AT. The last 0.5 mile brings you up to the summit of Wesser Bald at 4,627 feet. You might feel the wind pick up and the temperature drop as you reach the summit, although you might be sweating too much to notice! Enjoy spectacular 360-degree views

■ The Smokies from Wesser Bald

of the Nantahala Ridge, the Tennessee River Valley, and the Smoky and Balsam Mountains from the 30-foot fire tower. Be grateful that the U.S. Forest Service rebuilt the observation deck for hikers after the cabin was destroyed by arson in 1979, and then return the way you came.

Directions From Tsali Campground, turn right onto Tsali Road, then left onto NC 28 North. Continue 3.5 miles, and then turn right onto US 19 South/US 74 West. After 3.4 miles, turn left onto Wesser Creek Road and follow it 1.7 miles until it dead-ends at the trailhead.

Ledbetter Creek Adventure   *Variable distances, creek hiking, waterfalls, cave*

Channel your inner child with one of the best creek hikes in the Southeast! From the parking lot, cross US 74/19 to head north on the Bartram Trail. The trail meanders through a field that gets a bit overgrown in the summer but is passable. At 0.5 mile, you'll reach a small bridge. Splash through Ledbetter Creek upstream, carefully maneuvering over beautiful rock cascades as the creek tumbles down on its journey to the Nantahala River.

At 0.3 mile upstream, scramble up a cavelike hole on the right side of the ridge, emerging like a Bartramesque explorer above to gaze down at Ledbetter's cascades and pools. Bring your common sense and shoes that have a sturdy grip and can get wet for this hike.

Young or unsteady explorers can enjoy splashing in the creek close to the bridge. It's plenty scenic there too, so no need to compromise safety for the sake of adventure. Be sure to practice Leave No Trace ethics by traveling on durable surfaces and avoiding tromping on delicate flora as you splash upstream.

Directions From Tsali Campground, turn right onto Tsali Road, then left onto NC 28 North. Continue 3.5 miles, and then turn right onto US 19 South/US 74 West. Once you pass the Nantahala Outdoor Center, continue 6.8 miles. Parking for the trailhead is on the left.

PADDLING ⊗

WHITEWATER

Nantahala River *8-mile run, 2 hours, Class I–III, put in at Duke Power access, take out at Nantahala Outdoor Center (NOC)*

There's something mysteriously alluring about the Nantahala River. The lower stretch runs alongside the well-traveled US 74/19, but when you're enveloped in mist rising up from the water toward the steep canyon walls looming above you in this "land of the noonday sun," you're too enamored with your surroundings to even notice the traffic.

■ Nantahala River at NOC

The Nanty is an ideal introduction to whitewater paddling, with just enough action to keep the trip exciting but nothing that will terrify the young or inexperienced. Numerous outfitters offer guided trips, and semiexperienced paddlers can rent an inflatable kayak or a small raft and guide themselves through the mostly Class I–II rapids. Watch out for Little Wesser Falls, the one Class III, right before the takeout. If you're wary of too much excitement, there's an opportunity to take out before the falls.

More experienced canoeists and kayakers will love the challenge of surfing the plentiful holes and shooting this dam-fed river's boulder-strewn rapids. If you're piloting your own boat, arrive at the put-in before the 9 a.m. dam release to avoid much of the raft traffic. If you need a river run refuel, park your boat at Pizza by the River, located on river right.

The water in the Nantahala stays around 50°F year-round, and most outfitters will provide dry tops or rent wetsuits to chill-prone paddlers. Many outfitters also offer shuttles for a nominal charge. *Note:* Duke Energy does not schedule releases November–mid-March, except for a few days before January 1. The release schedule is available at duke-energy.com.

Directions to put-in From Tsali Campground, turn right onto Tsali Road, then left onto NC 28 north. Continue 3.5 miles, and then turn right onto US 19 South/US 74 West. Pass NOC and follow US 74/19 upriver 8 miles and turn left just below the power station at the junction of US 19 and Wayah Road. Public put-in is on the left. Purchase your $1 U.S. Forest Service daily fee permit at NOC.

Directions to takeout Follow directions to NOC above. If you're paddling your own boat, you can take out on the river right just above Wesser Falls or below the falls on river left, past the steel bridge at NOC. Don't shoot past the NOC takeout—just below is the deadly Class VI Big Wesser Falls.

Tuckasegee River *6.5-mile run, 1.5 hours, Class I–II+, put in at the CJ Harris Boating Access Area, take out at Smoky Mountain River Adventures*

Our favorite run on this family-friendly river begins in the quaint, artsy mountain town of Dillsboro, just under the US 441 bridge. Here, the river flows for 6.5 miles downstream to outfitters' takeouts on river right, with almost nonstop Class I and II+ whitewater fun that's ideal for rafts, kayaks, and even open canoes, if you've got the chops. We only got a *little* water over the side of our boat the last time we ran this section. We recommend dropping off your boat and gear at the put-in, and then driving north on US 441 to Smoky Mountain River Adventures (about 20 minutes from Tsali), where you can catch a shuttle to the put-in for $5.

Directions to put-in From Tsali Campground, turn right onto Tsali Road, then left onto NC 28 south. Continue 3.5 miles, and then turn left onto US 19 North/US 74 East, which eventually becomes US 74 East/US 441 South. You'll see the outfitters and takeout 300 yards past Uncle Bill's Flea Market on the right. Continue south and take the US 441 South exit toward Dillsboro. Continue 0.8 mile. At the bottom of the hill, turn left at the traffic light toward downtown Dillsboro, and then take the first two right turns to the gravel parking area and boat launch along Scott Creek. Experienced boaters can put in about 0.25 mile upriver to test their mettle on the Dillsboro Drop, a Class III ledge that was exposed with the removal of the Dillsboro dam. To get to this put-in, go straight through the traffic light on US 441 and turn left on North River Road. The put-in for this section is about 0.5 mile on the right.

Nantahala Outdoor Center *13077 W. US 19, Bryson City; 828-366-7502; noc.com*

If you want to do just about anything on the Nantahala, NOC will hook you up. Rentals, instructions, and guide services; park and take out here. Hourly shuttles for $7.

Rolling Thunder River Company *10160 US 19, Bryson City; 800-408-7238*

An affordable, high-quality option for guided trips and rentals.

Smoky Mountain River Adventures *5036 US 74, Whittier; 828-586-5285; raftingwithmykids.com*

Raft and inflatable kayak rentals, shuttles, and parking at the takeout.

FLATWATER

If you're camping at Tsali, there's enjoyable flatwater boating along the coves of Fontana Lake. Take a left out of the campground to reach the boat ramp in about a minute. You can also put in at the Fingerlake Day Use Area, near where NC 28 crosses the Nantahala River. This is a popular spot for whitewater paddlers to play and practice their rolls, and SUP-ers enjoy the wide-open stretch of calm water.

OTHER ADVENTURES ⊕

Great Smoky Mountains Railroad
226 Everett St., Bryson City; 828-586-8811; gsmr.com

You've traveled by foot, boat, and bike . . . now explore the Nantahala Valley by train! Enjoy open-air gondola seating in good weather or stay toasty and dry in a closed car when the weather is less than inviting.

All aboard the train.

MAPS 📖

Nantahala Gorge National Geographic's Trails Illustrated *Nantahala and Cullasaja Gorge* area map. Both the Wesser Bald and Ledbetter Creek hikes are on this map, as is the trailhead for the GSMNP hikes. Available in local outfitters or online at natgeomaps.com/nantahala-and-cullasaja-gorges-nantahala-national-forest.

Great Smoky Mountains National Park National Geographic's Trails Illustrated *Clingman's Dome, Cataloochee* area map is rendered in sufficient detail for hiking and navigating in the Deep Creek area. This map is available locally in outfitters and online at natgeomaps.com/cades-cove-elkmont-great-smoky-mountains-national-park.

FOOD AND DRINK 🍴

Nantahala Brewing Company *61 Depot St., Bryson City; 828-488-2337; nantahalabrewingcompany.com*

Nantahala Brewing Company boasts an impressive array of beers regularly on tap, including six flagship beers. You can't go wrong with the Noon Day IPA, even if you're usually not an IPA fan.

The Bistro at the Everett Hotel *16 Everett St., Bryson City; 888-488-1934; theeveretthotel.com*

This "social mountain house" is both a coffee shop and restaurant with cabin-chic ambiance, extensive beer and wine selections, and a seasonal menu with Mediterranean-influenced tapas, locally caught trout, a wide variety of crepes, and vegetarian options.

River's End Restaurant *Located at NOC, overlooking the Nantahala River; 828-488-2176; noc.com*

Casual American-style food done well with good-size portions for hungry adventurers. Our recommendation: start with the black bean chili and ask for jalapeños—it's the fastest way to warm up after paddling down the river!

GEAR AND RESUPPLY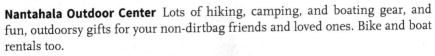

Nantahala Outdoor Center Lots of hiking, camping, and boating gear, and fun, outdoorsy gifts for your non-dirtbag friends and loved ones. Bike and boat rentals too.

Bryson City Outdoors *169 Main St., Bryson City; 828-342-6444; brysoncityoutdoors.com*

Small but continually growing supply of camping and paddling gear (rentals too) and the coolest outdoor T-shirts. Employees are happy to talk about the area and offer adventure suggestions.

Crowders Mountain

CHARLOTTE

Charlotte is full of one-stop adventure shopping. If we could sleep at the U.S. National Whitewater Center, we'd never leave. With Olympic-caliber and family-friendly paddling on their man-made recirculating river, 30 miles of biking and hiking trails, climbing, ziplining, and riverside dining, it's like Disney World for outdoors lovers. The McDowell Nature Center and Preserve is a 1,000-plus-acre gem, and offers camping, hiking, and paddling just 30 minutes from downtown. Commune with nature by bike on the McMullen Greenway, then go peak bagging at Crowders Mountain, where climbers and hikers can both score panoramic views of the Piedmont.

Areas included: Catawba River, Crowders Mountain State Park, Lake Wylie, McDowell Nature Center and Preserve, McMullen Greenway, Sherman Branch Mountain Biking Park, U.S. National Whitewater Center

Adventures: Camping, mountain and road biking, hiking, climbing, flatwater and whitewater paddling, challenge course, ziplining

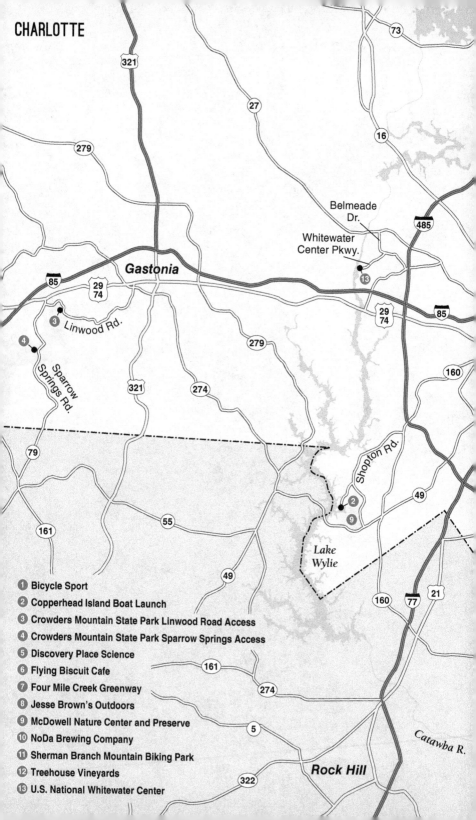

CHARLOTTE

321

27

73

16

279

485

Belmeade Dr.

Whitewater Center Pkwy.

⑬

Gastonia

85

29 74

③ Linwood Rd.

29 74

85

④

160

Sparrow Springs Rd.

279

321

274

Shopton Rd.

79

49

②
⑨

55

160

49

Lake Wylie

161

77

21

① Bicycle Sport

② Copperhead Island Boat Launch

③ Crowders Mountain State Park Linwood Road Access

④ Crowders Mountain State Park Sparrow Springs Access

⑤ Discovery Place Science

⑥ Flying Biscuit Cafe

⑦ Four Mile Creek Greenway

⑧ Jesse Brown's Outdoors

⑨ McDowell Nature Center and Preserve

⑩ NoDa Brewing Company

⑪ Sherman Branch Mountain Biking Park

⑫ Treehouse Vineyards

⑬ U.S. National Whitewater Center

161

274

5

Catawba R.

Rock Hill

322

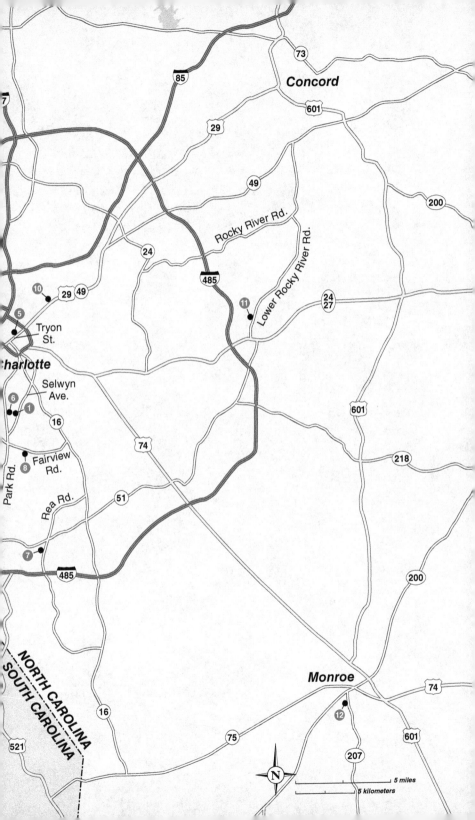

TOP PICK

MCDOWELL NATURE CENTER AND PRESERVE (MECKLENBURG COUNTY)

15222 S. York Road, Charlotte; 704-583-1284; charmeck.org. $19+/night, open year-round, 56 sites, reservations accepted, picnic table, fire ring, flush toilets, hot showers, some sites share central water, hookups available, firewood and ice available for purchase, nature center, boat launch

■ Plenty of room for toys at McDowell Campground

Mecklenburg County touts the McDowell Nature Center and Preserve as the Great Urban Escape, but we think it's worth a visit even if you're not trying to get away from city life. Located on the banks of Lake Wylie, the preserve has a great campground that sits on a wooded ridge. RVs have their own area, so tent campers don't have to set up alongside massive motorhomes. You actually don't even have to own a tent to camp here, as the rent-a-tent sites are equipped with a sturdy 12-by-12-foot tent. Our favorite sites are at the back of the D loop. These sites are level, private, and can fit one medium to large tent. In the winter you might notice hints of development in the distance, but you'll also get great sunset views.

Directions From Charlotte, take I-77 South to Exit 1. At the end of the exit ramp, turn right onto Westinghouse Blvd. In 1.5 miles, turn left onto NC 49 S/S Tryon St. Follow NC 49 for 5.5 miles, then turn right onto McDowell Parkway, following signs for the nature preserve.

■ Lake Wylie

BACKUP BASE CAMP

Crowders Mountain State Park (NC State Parks) *522 Park Office Ln., Kings Mountain; 704-853-5375; ncparks.gov/crowders-mountain-state-park. $10/night, open year-round, 10 sites, reservations accepted, walk-in sites (1-mile hike), picnic table, fire ring, pit toilets, central water*

It's a 1-mile hike to the campsites, but you'll be rewarded for the trek with solitude and trail access right outside your tent door.

INDOOR LODGING

Treehouse Vineyards *301 Bay St., Monroe; 704-283-4208; treehousevineyards.com. $150–$350/night, queen bed and sleeper sofa, efficiency kitchen, heat and air-conditioning, private bath, no pets*

This isn't your kid's tree house. Comfy beds, amazing vineyard views, spacious decks, and wine tastings are just a short stroll away. About 45 minutes southeast of Charlotte, it's a bit out of the way, but did we mention that you get to sleep in a tree house?

BIKING ❷

MOUNTAIN BIKING

U.S. National Whitewater Center Loop *16 miles, 2–3 hours, beginner–advanced, slalom course, jumps, rock gardens, berms, lots of loop options*

With your $5/car entrance fee, you have access to almost 30 miles of primo mountain bike and hiking trails at the USNWC. With beginner, intermediate, and advanced trails, the center has something for everyone. No bike? Adult and child bikes are available to rent. The trail system comprises more than a dozen trails, most under 3 miles, and connector trails make it easy to ride loops of varying distances. All trail junctions are well signed. Purchase maps for $2 at the outfitter's store or print one from usnwc.org. Check the website for trail closings. Our go-to loop hits up all three levels of trails, but the connector trails make it easy to skip or add trails to your ride.

■ Catching air at USNWC

Ride to the back of the main parking lot, then head up the gravel road to the 3-mile Lake Trail (beginner). This easy trail is a great warm-up and is also popular with families and hikers, so take it easy out there, tiger. Cross under the power lines to reach the trailhead for the South Main Trail and enjoy the ride downhill. Stay to the left past the aerial park and junction with the North Main Connector Trails, then turn left onto the 1-mile Carpet Trail (advanced). Yes, there is carpet on the trail and you'll appreciate it as you climb a tricky switchback. At the end of the Carpet Trail, turn left back onto South Main, then left again onto the 0.6-mile Tower 93 Trail (advanced). If you're not into catching air at high speeds, take it easy on the back side of this trail. Turn left onto South Main and left again onto the 0.5-mile Wedge Trail (intermediate), which has a mellow climb and fast descent. Head left on South Main, then left onto the 1-mile Goat Hill Trail (advanced).

■ USNWC Trail

For some extra technical climbing and descending, take the left option at the top of the first climb. Think like a billy goat and keep the rubber side down on the screaming descents, jumps, and rollers. Turn left onto South Main, then turn right onto the 0.6-mile Weigh Station Trail (intermediate) for a moderately hilly, rocky, and rooty cruise. Turn right onto South Main, then turn left onto the 1-mile Toilet Bowl Trail (advanced). This trail starts with one of the best descents in the system, chock full of berms, jumps, and fast straightaways. Turn left onto South Main and continue to the 0.25-mile Slalom Course. Take a few laps around the course, then turn right on South Main and follow the power lines back to the parking lot. For an additional 5.7 miles, continue past the parking lot on the left and turn right onto the recently built East Main Trail (intermediate). You'll have several bailout options on this trail, but the last section is the longest. Just something to keep in mind if you're feeling more like a post-ride riverside beer than additional miles.

Directions From McDowell Nature Center and Preserve, turn left onto McDowell Parkway, then left onto NC 49 North. In 2.3 miles, turn left onto NC 160 North/Steele Creek Road. Travel for 4.8 miles, then merge onto I-485 Inner (North). Continue 7.2 miles, then take Exit 12 for Moores Chapel Road. At the traffic circle, take the first exit onto Moores Chapel Road, then turn right onto Rhyne Road. Quickly turn left onto Belmeade Dr. Travel for 1.2 miles, then turn left onto Whitewater Center Parkway. After 0.9 mile, veer right to continue on Whitewater Center Parkway, then turn right onto U.S. National Whitewater Center Dr.

Sherman Branch *11 miles of trails, beginner–intermediate, multiple loop options, berms, whoop-de-dos, jumps, skinnies, rock gardens, easy exit options*

Thanks to the foresight and relentless work of the Tarheel Trailblazers, this trail system contains the Queen City's most beloved mountain biking hot spots. The system is made up of three trails, with connector trails that make it easy to ride shorter or longer loops. An access trail zigzags across the main trails, in case you need an easy out back to the parking lot. There are technical man-made features and skill-testing rock gardens, but even beginner riders with some experience can ride almost everything here. No water at the trailhead; portable toilets available. Check tarheeltrailblazers.com for trail closings. Recommended direction is clockwise and the trails are well blazed.

Start on the 6.9-mile Main Loop near the kiosk. The Main Loop has lots of long, smooth, pedal-to-the-metal sections that launch you into perfectly bermed turns. There are a few mild climbs, but nothing gut-busting.

Around mile 0.5, a connector trail leads to the 1.9-mile Roller Coaster Trail. Roller Coaster, named for its seemingly endless whoop-de-dos, is a more advanced trail. There are short but steep climbs, tight and twisty turns, and hang-on-tight descents.

At the end of your Roller Coaster ride, you can continue on the Main Loop or take the access road back to the parking lot. If you stay on the main loop, you can take the connector trail to the 2.1-mile Big Lake Trail. Big Lake has the hardest climbs, the biggest roots, and the trickiest rock gardens of the three trails. You can also peel off onto the access road to doubletrack it back to your car or just continue on the Main Trail to finish your ride.

> **Directions** From McDowell Nature Center and Preserve, turn left onto McDowell Parkway, then left onto NC 49 North. Travel 6.5 miles, then turn right onto the I-485 South ramp. Continue on I-485 for 28 miles, then take Exit 41 for NC 24/27. Turn left onto NC 24/27 East. After 0.8 mile, turn left onto Rocky Church Road. The park is 1 mile on the left.

ROAD BIKING

Four Mile Creek/Lower McAlpine/McMullen Creek Greenway *11.6-mile out-and-back, 1–2 hours, easy, wetlands, great blue heron rookery, boardwalks*

This 5.8-mile (one way) path—referred to as just McMullen by locals—is a relaxing way to cruise through some scenic landscapes on Charlotte's south side. A mix of pavement, gravel, and boardwalk, this is a popular route for runners, cyclists, families, and ramblers, so think party pace, not peloton.

As the names suggest, you'll ride alongside creeks and through wetlands for much of the ride. The Four Mile Creek Greenway is home to a great blue heron rookery, so watch for nests (while you're stopped).

We recommend starting at the end of the Four Mile Greenway on Bevington Place. Park at the lot across the street from the Shops of Piper Glen, where you can pick up the usual urban refreshments (Starbucks, Jamba Juice, Trader Joe's) to start or end your ride. The Greenway changes names a few times throughout your ride, but it's one continuous trail. Four Mile Creek turns into Lower McAlpine just before mile 2; after crossing under I-485, it changes to the McMullen Creek Greenway.

Directions From McDowell Nature Center and Preserve, turn left onto McDowell Parkway, then left again onto NC 49 North. After 6.5 miles, turn right onto I-485 South. Continue on I-485 Outer 9 miles, then take Exit 64A to merge onto NC 51 North. Drive 3.4 miles, then turn right onto Elm Lane. In 0.4 mile, turn left onto Bevington Place. Parking lot is on the right.

Bicycle Sport *2916 Selwyn Ave., Charlotte; 704-335-0323; bicyclesport.com*

You'll feel at home as soon as you walk in the door, and if there's something your bike needs, they'll have it. They're big supporters of the local bike scene, from family-friendly cruising to the racing circuit.

HIKING ⬤

Kingfisher Loop at McDowell Nature Center and Preserve *2.5-mile loop, 1 hour, easy, lake views, piers, wetlands, nature center, free map available at office*

OK, so the hiking at McDowell won't be the wildest experience of your life, but the trails are worth a stroll. Young hikers will love the pit stops: observation decks, a floating pier, and the nature center.

■ Crowders Mountain State Park

Start on the Kingfisher Trail (blue triangle blazes) from the primitive camping parking lot. At 0.1 mile, a short spur trail on the left leads to a pier. The trail soon meets the Chestnut Trail; continue on Kingfisher. At the gravel road, follow the road for a short distance. Watch for steps on the left that lead back to the Kingfisher Trail. After 0.1 mile, you'll reach the pier.

Follow the sidewalk through the Memorial Garden, then head back into the woods, following signs for the Kingfisher Trail. The trail turns left and heads gently uphill. If you didn't make a beach stop earlier, lots of short footpaths lead down to the water from here. Follow the trail signs and continue across a footbridge, then pass a picnic area. At the gravel road, turn right and walk through the parking lot. Continue on the road, watching for the Cove Trail on the left. The Cove Trail might feel familiar, as it also follows the shores of Lake Wylie, and then passes another picnic area, but who can possibly complain about too many lake views and picnic spots?

Lake Wylie

Just past the picnic pavilion you'll reach a parking lot. Cross the parking lot and continue onto the paved Four Seasons Trail for a short distance, then turn right onto the Pine Hollow Trail (yellow square blazes), which leads to the nature center. If it's open, stop in and see what animals are hanging out that day. Pass the fire ring, then turn left. At the junction with the connector trail (white blazes), continue straight on the connector. You'll soon meet up with the Chestnut Trail (red circle blazes), which leads to the office. Take the road back to the parking lot or your campsite.

Directions Follow directions in the McDowell Nature Center and Preserve campground section on page 62.

Rocktop Loop at Crowders Mountain State Park *6-mile lollipop loop, 3 hours, moderate–strenuous, summit, Piedmont views, cliffs*

You'll regularly hear Crowders Mountain referred to as Crowded Mountain by locals, but there's a reason the masses flock to its peaks. At 1,625 feet high, Crowders Mountain is the best mountain experience you can get just 30 miles from downtown Charlotte. While the park does get crowded, it's not impossible to find some quiet time on the trail, even on a busy weekend. Hike early morning or late afternoon to make sure you don't get turned away if the parking lot is full.

There are two access points to the park. This hike starts at the Sparrow Springs Visitor Center, where you can grab a map. Head past the visitor center to the Crowders Trail (white diamond blazes). At 0.2 mile, you'll reach a junction with the Pinnacle Trail. Keep right to continue on the Crowders Trail. When the trail crosses the paved Sparrow Springs Road, veer right onto the Rocktop Trail

■ The Backside Trail leads to the summit of Crowders Mountain.

(red circle blazes). Scramble over rocks, boulders, and fallen trees as you ascend to your first views of the valley below. Continue on the Rocktop Trail past the junction with the Tower Trail, an old gravel roadbed that is still used by vehicles to reach the radio towers on top of Crowders Mountain. From the towers, head downhill on the Backside Trail (orange hexagon blazes) to the summit of Crowders Mountain and soak up 25-mile views of the Piedmont. This is the most popular spot on the trail, but there's plenty of rocky ridgeline to explore on top of the sheer 150-foot cliffs.

When you're ready to exchange views for solitude, head down the 336 wooden steps behind the cliffs. Just before you reach the Linville Road parking area, turn right onto the Tower Trail (blue square blazes). This old roadbed is lightly trafficked and the surrounding woods feel especially cool and quiet after the busy summit. Follow the Tower Trail 1.7 miles until you return to the Rocktop Trail. Turn left on Rocktop and follow it to the Crowders Trail. Take the Crowders Trail back to the trailhead.

Directions From McDowell Nature Center and Preserve, turn left onto McDowell Parkway, then turn right onto NC 49 South (which becomes SC 49 South). Continue 4.2 miles. Stay straight to follow SC 557 for 2.3 miles, then veer right onto State Road S-46-27. Stay on State Road S-46-27 for 5.4 miles, then continue onto NC 42/Ferguson Ridge Road. After 2.8 miles, turn left onto Crowders Creek Road. Travel 0.7 mile, then turn right onto Freedom Mill Road. After 3.4 miles, turn left onto Sparrow Springs Road and continue 1 mile. Park entrance is on the left.

CLIMBING 🧗

Crowders Mountain State Park *Single-pitch top-rope and sport climbing, 5.4–5.13, best in fall, winter, and spring, free public access, registration required*

Climbers of all skill levels have plenty of options at Crowders. Most of the main crags face southeast, making it best on cool summer mornings, and fall, winter, and spring. (The park is less crowded then too.) Nearly all the climbing areas are at the top of Crowders Mountain, which is most easily reached via the 0.8-mile Backside Trail at the Linwood Road access. The Backside Trail heads up a set of stairs to the top of the cliff area. From here, turn left (northeast) and follow a climber's trail to a steep gully on the right (southeast) side of the mountain that leads to the bottom of David's Castle (on left). To anchor at the top of Practice Wall, continue straight at the top of the Backside Trail stairs, past the top of Practice Wall on the left. Turn left on an access trail to reach the bottom of the wall. If you get to the radio towers, you've gone too far.

■ Getting a feel for the rock at Crowders Mountain

You can also reach the bottom of Practice Wall by turning right at the bottom of the gully, southwest of David's Castle. Almost all of the routes here can be easily top-roped. Many routes on David's Castle have bolts for sport climbing.

Crack and chimney lovers can jam their hands, feet, and bodies in the abundant fissures in the quartzite face of Crowders. Classic routes like Gastonia Crack (5.4) and Burn Crack (5.10c) on Practice Wall, and Caterpillar (5.7 chimney) and Instant Karma Direct (5.10d corner/crack) on David's Castle are some of our favorite lines. Yon Lambert and Harrison Shull's *Selected Climbs in North Carolina* describes routes on Practice Wall, David's Castle, Red Wall (northeast of David's Castle) and Hidden Wall (accessed from the visitor center).

Because of Crowders' proximity to Charlotte, you'll usually find other climbers who know the area well and can direct you to whatever you fancy. For an excellent overview of the climbing here, check out crowdersmountain.com, which has 2- and 3-D maps of the climbing areas. The visitor center has several climbing guides for sale, along with desk copies that you can peruse before heading out to the cliffs.

PADDLING ⊗

WHITEWATER

USNWC Whitewater Rafting *Class II–IV, recirculating man-made river, whitewater rafting, kayaking and SUP, clinics and lessons, open mid-March–October, activity pass purchase required*

While the Catawba River provides plenty of calm paddle opportunities around Charlotte, if you're craving fast water, hit up the USNWC. What this artificial recirculating river lacks in natural beauty, it makes up for in thrills.

The center offers numerous guided rafting trips, from Class II–III family rafting to the Class II–IV Rodeo Rafting, where you're just about guaranteed to swim at least once. Experienced paddlers with their own gear—kayak or SUP, paddle, skirt, PFD, and helmet—can hone their skills on the river with the purchase of a $25 day pass.

The river is divided into two channels. From the pool at the top, the channel on the left is the longer and easier of the two, with tons of Class II–III rapids. You could spend an entire afternoon playing in the eddies here, without having to worry about strainers or undercuts. Be warned: the eddies are fun but aggressive, and they can easily launch you back into the rapids you just conquered. The steeper, shorter channel on the right is the playground of Olympic kayakers and should only be attempted by extremely proficient paddlers. This channel has fast and furious nonstop Class III–IV rapids that don't let up until the end.

Want another run? Ride the conveyer belt to the start of the river. (Yes, we're serious.) Don't quite have the skills to take on the rapids? The center offers kayak and SUP instruction.

Directions See directions in the biking section, page 64.

■ Lake Wylie

FLATWATER

Lake Wylie Lake Wylie, a man-made lake straddling the North Carolina/South Carolina border, is fun for brand-new and experienced paddlers alike. We like to put in at the McDowell Nature Center and Preserve boat launch.

No boat? Contact Twisted Beaver River Adventures (877-745-1562, twistedriveradventures.com), which rents kayaks and canoes year-round. The preserve doesn't rent boats, but it does offer guided kayak tours in the spring and summer. You can also launch at the preserve's 14-acre Copperhead Island (15200 Soldier Road). It's a fun mini-adventure to paddle around the island, despite the ominous name. There's less boat traffic here than on other parts of the lake, and it's a great SUP spot. There are primitive campsites on Copperhead Island, but even if you're not camping, you can park your boat and explore the footpaths through the woods in a Tom Sawyer and Huck Finn-ish fashion.

Catawba River at the U.S. National Whitewater Center With the purchase of an activity pass, you'll have access to single and tandem sit-on-top kayaks and SUPs. These can be used on the languid section of the Catawba River that flows through the west side of the center. For just the $5 entrance fee, paddlers with their own boat can use the center's flatwater put-in on the river. There's a short portage to access the boat launch. You'll have a fair amount of company most nice weekends, but many paddlers stick close to the put-in. Unless the river is running unusually high, it's easy to paddle up or downriver to escape the crowds. Slip into one of the many coves, where you'll find more turtles, great blue herons, ospreys, and beavers than people.

VERTICAL ADVENTURES

U.S. National Whitewater Center

On top of one-stop paddling, hiking, and biking, the USNWC has about 101 ways to have fun in a harness. Between the three climbing walls, ziplines spanning over 1,000 feet, aerial challenge courses, and free jump platforms, pint-size adventurers through advanced climbers can get their adrenaline highs here. All aerial activities require an activity pass purchase.

If you're a serious climber, take on the Spire climbing wall. It's the most natural of the walls, with lead climbing options and boulder problems. For families, the Adventure Course is the Goldilocks of the aerial options. At 20 feet up, it's not too high or too low, and the treetop obstacles are just right for families.

■ Ziplines at USNWC

If you want a unique adventure, take the plunge on the Deep Water Solo Climbing Wall complex. With no ropes, no harnesses, and a 20-foot-deep pool, it's the perfect way to end your day with a splash.

MAPS

Maps for most of Charlotte's adventures are available at the facilities themselves and on their respective websites.

Lake Wylie Kingfisher's *Lake Wylie*. If you're sticking close to McDowell Nature Center and Preserve, you won't need a map, but if you want to explore more of the lake, it's a useful tool. Available for purchase at kfmaps.com/shop /lake-maps/lake-wylie-327.

RAINY DAY

Discovery Place Science and Nature Museum *301 N. Tryon St., Charlotte; 704-372-6261; discoveryplace.org*

While there's plenty of kid-friendly fun at these two science hubs, there's lots for mature adventurers to enjoy too. The science museum has the more grown-up vibe—who doesn't love an IMAX theater?—but we're sure you'll expand your outdoor IQ at the nature center too. Discovery Place Science: $17/adult, $13/ child. Discovery Place Nature: $8/person.

FOOD AND DRINK

Flying Biscuit Cafe *4241 Park Road, Charlotte; 704-714-3400; flyingbiscuit.com*

Say yes to the moon-dusted potatoes. We still don't know exactly what moon dust is, but we assume it's legal, despite being addicting. Even the salads come with a biscuit, so you can get the best of all meals in one sitting. Breakfast served all day too.

Flying Biscuit Cafe

NoDa Brewing *2921 N. Tryon St., Charlotte; 704-900-6851; nodabrewing.com*

Ask your Charlotte friends if they've been to NoDa and they'll probably laugh . . . because everyone goes to NoDa! The Coco Loco chocolate-coconut porter is available year-round. For such a brave brewing move, we salute you, NoDa.

GEAR AND RESUPPLY 🛒

There are several super-markets, chain restaurants, and drugstores less than 10 minutes away from the McDowell Nature Center and Preserve on NC 49/ South Tryon Road. If you need to pick up outdoor gear, there's a newly expanded outfitter store at the USNWC, and an REI and a Great

■ USNWC

Outdoor Provision Company within half an hour of the preserve. If you like your outdoor stores local, check out Jesse Brown's Outdoors.

Jesse Brown's Outdoors *4732 Sharon Road; 704-556-0020; jessebrowns.com*

Jesse Brown's has been selling outdoor gear to local adventurers since the 1970s. You'll find your usual assortment of the trendy and the practical, and the friendly gear-junkie staff is happy to answer questions.

Neusiock Trail

CROATAN NATIONAL FOREST

The Croatan National Forest is an ecosystem smorgasbord. Coast, swamp, salt marsh, longleaf pine savannah, maritime forest: it's all here. For your coastal paddling fix, make like a sea turtle and paddle to the wild and pristine Bear Island. Or, for something completely different, head into the swamp and paddle through the blackwater of the mysterious White Oak River. Ready to hike? The 21-mile Neusiock Trail offers some of the best and most diverse coastal hiking we've done. Spoiler alert: there are (gentle) hills. And before your mountain bike gets all huffy, you can hit the trails on two wheels at Flanners Beach Campground. The nearby town of New Bern has a very healthy road bike scene, so skinny tires are welcome too.

Areas included: Bear Island, Croatan National Forest, Hammocks Beach State Park, New Bern, White Oak River

Adventures: Camping, mountain and road biking, hiking, paddling

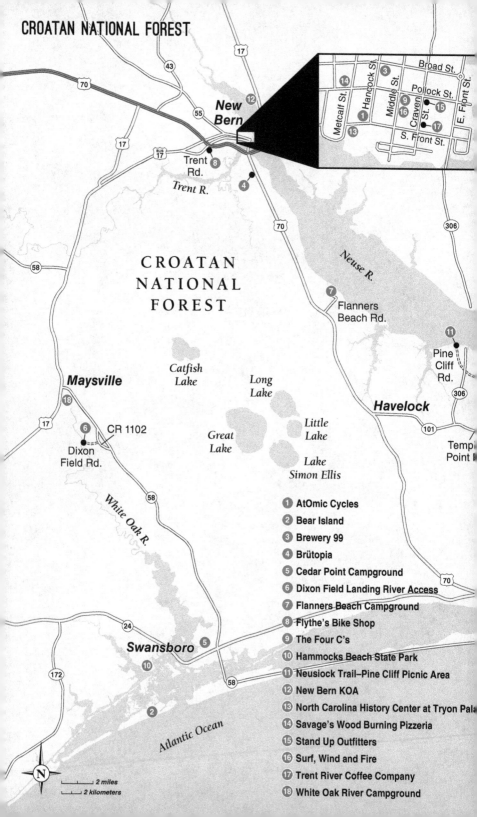

CROATAN NATIONAL FOREST

CROATAN NATIONAL FOREST

New Bern

Maysville

Havelock

Swansboro

Atlantic Ocean

1 AtOmic Cycles
2 Bear Island
3 Brewery 99
4 Brütopia
5 Cedar Point Campground
6 Dixon Field Landing River Access
7 Flanners Beach Campground
8 Flythe's Bike Shop
9 The Four C's
10 Hammocks Beach State Park
11 Neusiock Trail–Pine Cliff Picnic Area
12 New Bern KOA
13 North Carolina History Center at Tryon Pala
14 Savage's Wood Burning Pizzeria
15 Stand Up Outfitters
16 Surf, Wind and Fire
17 Trent River Coffee Company
18 White Oak River Campground

TOP PICK

FLANNERS BEACH CAMPGROUND (U.S. FOREST SERVICE) *300 Flanners Beach Road, New Bern; 252-638-5628; www.fs.usda.gov. $12/night, open March–November (call for exact dates), 40 sites, reservations accepted, picnic table, fire ring, lantern pole, flush toilets, hot showers, central water, 24 sites with electric available for an additional $5/night.*

We're die-hard tent campers. However, we think that the sites with electrical hookups at Flanners Beach Campground (also called Neuse River Campground) are better than the nonelectric tent sites. This isn't because we have a lot of equipment that requires electricity—although, the next time we camp in August, we're bringing a fan and a long extension cord—but because the electric sites are bigger, more private, and have ample tree canopy. If shade and solitude are high on your list of campsite essentials, the extra $5 a night is worth it.

■ Sunset over the Neuse River behind our campsite

That said, the nonelectric sites have all the basics, and the ones toward the back of the loop get first-class Neuse River views with a nightly sunset show. Grab site 28 or 29, if you can. If you get creative with the lantern poles and the handful of trees, you can hang a hammock or tarp in these sites. They also stay pretty dry, even after a hard rain, and the paved path that circumnavigates the campground runs right behind them. Just beyond the path, you can scramble down to the broad Neuse River and enjoy a small, quiet stretch of beach. There's also a bigger beach area a short walk away, down the stairs from the picnic area.

There's no dedicated boat launch at Flanners Beach, but you can carry a small craft down to the river, and there's a myriad of paddling opportunities within a half-hour drive.

Directions From New Bern, travel southeast about 10 miles on US 70 East. Turn left onto Flanners Beach Road (SR 1107) and travel about 0.5 mile to the recreation area.

From Morehead City, travel northwest on US 70 West about 20 miles. Turn right onto Flanners Beach Road (SR 1107) and travel about 0.5 mile to the recreation area.

Cedar Point Campground (U.S. Forest Service) *391 VFW Road, Cedar Point; 252-638-5628; www.fs.usda.gov. $27/night, open year-round, 40 sites, reservations accepted for some sites, picnic table, fire ring, lantern hook, flush toilets, hot showers, central water, all sites have electric, dump station*

Paddling the White Oak River

Located in the southwestern part of the Croatan National Forest near Bogue Banks, Swansboro, and Emerald Isle, Cedar Point also makes a great Croatan base camp. You're only a few miles away from Emerald Isle's beautiful beaches, and you can paddle the White Oak River from the campground's boat launch; also, the trailhead for the short but sweet Cedar Point Tideland Trail is right by the boat launch. All these attractions are just a few minutes away from your campsite.

INDOOR LODGING

New Bern KOA Camping Cabins
1565 B St., New Bern; 252-638-2556; koa.com/campgrounds/new-bern. $39–$89/night, cabins sleep up to six, twin, full, and queen beds, heat and air-conditioning, amenities vary

While the Disneyesque camping at KOAs isn't quite our style, their log cabins are cozy, clean, and comfortable. Accommodations range from the basic (a dry place to sleep, on a real bed, with shared bathroom facilities) to the deluxe (a full kitchen and a patio). Dog friendly too!

BIKING

MOUNTAIN BIKING

Coastal mountain biking isn't a complete oxymoron, but be realistic. Don't expect huge climbs and descents, and remember that sand isn't the most forgiving trail surface, especially when braking at high speeds. But the loop around Flanners Beach Campground is definitely worth a spin and also makes a great hike or trail run.

Flanners Beach Campground Loop *5.5 miles, 1 hour, easy–moderate, flowy, gentle hills, well-built trails*

This loop, best conquered counterclockwise (it's easier to read the trail signs that way), starts at the far end of the Flanners Beach Campground picnic area. From the paved campground path, veer left at the generic FOREST SERVICE TRAIL sign. These signs mark the first part of the trail before it meets Flanners Beach Road. This section of trail is well-designed, classic singletrack, and you'll even get a few mild climbs and descents as it carves through a bluff above the Neuse River. You'll roll over a few rooty sections; otherwise, it's a smooth, beginner-friendly ride. Just a heads up, though: there are some tight switchback turns that can sneak up on you just as you hit full speed on some straight sections. Look ahead and use this opportunity to hone those tight-turning skills!

■ Flanners Beach Campground Loop

Around mile 2.2, the trail crosses Flanners Beach Road. While we're not trying to imply that the second half of the trail is evil, the two sections do have a Jekyll and Hyde–like quality. Still under construction, the second half is perfectly rideable, just more rough and rugged. You'll encounter bigger roots, blowdowns, more twists and turns, and flooded sections after it rains. You can carefully ride through these wet sections, but you'll feel pretty swamped by the end. The last time we rode here this part wasn't signed, but it was well marked by lots of white spray-painted arrows. Not pretty, but it gets the job done! At the T-intersection with the gravel trail, turn right. After about 0.5 mile of fun singletrack, you'll encounter numerous side trails. Veer left, then left again, and enjoy the fastest section of the trail back to the paved path in the campground.

Directions Follow directions to Flanners Beach Campground (see page 77).

ROAD BIKING

There are tons of routes in this area, including 100-plus-mile epics and gravel road grinders. Check out the local shops for details on events, group rides, and local conditions. If you just want a nice, simple ride from your tent, the ride below fits the bill.

Flanners Beach to New Bern *30 miles round-trip, 1.5–2 hours, easy–moderate, out-and-back, country roads, river views*

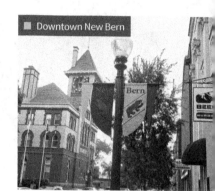
■ Downtown New Bern

This ride utilizes some of the local Thursday night ride route, heading into downtown New Bern for a snack by the water, a coffee break, or a brewery stop.

- Starting at Flanners Beach Campground, ride southwest on Flanners Beach Road.
- Mile 1: Turn right onto the access road, just before the intersection with US 70.
- Mile 1.2: Turn left onto Catfish Lake Road.
- Mile 1.25: Cross US 70, then turn immediately right onto County Line Road.
- Mile 3.5: Veer right onto Wilcox Road.
- Mile 4.75: Left onto Waterscape Way.
- Mile 6.9: Take the second exit from the traffic circle onto Landscape Way.
- Mile 7.6: Right at the T-intersection onto Old Airport Road.
- Mile 9.1: Right at another T-intersection onto Taberna Circle.
- Mile 9.5: Left onto Taberna Way.
- Mile 10.25: Right onto Old Airport Road (becomes Lagoon Road).
- Mile 11.9: Right onto Airport Road.
- Mile 12: Left onto Terminal Dr.
- Mile 12.35: Right onto Airline Dr.
- Mile 12.5: Left onto Williams Road.
- Mile 12.9: Right onto Howell Road.
- Mile 14.2: Left onto East Front St. Continue over the Trent River and stop at Union Park for a view of the Neuse and Trent Rivers' confluence.

If you're feeling the need for caffeine, head to Trent River Coffee Company, where you can juice up with baked goods and espresso just like the Europeans do. Turn left onto South Front St., just past the park, then turn right onto

Craven St. For a different kind of hydration, Brewery 99 is located just two blocks west and north of the coffee shop on the corner of Hancock and Broad Sts. Just remember that you need to ride back, so imbibe responsibly or arrange a pickup. Follow the route back in reverse.

AtOmic Cycles *504 S. Front St., New Bern; 252-633-2242; atomiccyclesnbnc.com*

Road bikers, rejoice: you've found your people. Talk to the owner Tom about the local scene if you get a chance. Full-service shop; check for weekend group rides (these are serious rides) on their website.

Flythe's Bike Shop *2411 Trent Road, New Bern; 252-638-1544; flythebikeshop.com*

Friendly full-service shop. Cruiser rentals (good for tooling around town) and weekend 8:30 a.m. no-drop rides.

HIKING ●

Neusiock Trail *7.5-mile out-and-back, 3–4 hours, easy, beach, mangroves, pocosin bogs, cypress swamps, shelter, Mountains-to-Sea Trail*

Want to be at the mountains and the beach at the same time? Well, we can't make that happen—at least not in North Carolina—but you'll get the feel of both on the Neusiock Trail, the best (and longest) trail in Eastern North Carolina that you've probably never heard of. Located entirely in the Croatan National Forest, this 21-mile footpath runs from the Pine Cliff Picnic Area to Oyster Point Campground and is part of the 900-mile Mountains-to-Sea Trail. If a 20-plus-mile, end-to-end hike isn't on the weekend agenda, check out the section from the Pine Cliff Picnic Area to the Copperhead Landing shelter.

To start, head past the bathrooms and the pavilion, with the Neuse River on your right, then veer left to the trailhead. The trail bisects two worlds here. On

Neusiock Trail

the right, you have the sandy banks of the Neuse River, lined with knobby-kneed bald cypress trees. To the left, there's the cool, deep pine forest. There's no getting lost on the trail, which is well blazed and has signs that mark mileage and major turns. An equestrian trail ventures off the main path, but it's also distinctly marked. In the first 1.5 miles, you'll hike dirt paths and sandy beach; then, the path leaves the river. Continue hiking up and over small rolling hills and pass through strands of hardwood and pine forests, cypress swamps, and across a boardwalk through a freshwater wetland. At 3.75 miles, you'll reach the Copperhead Landing shelter. There's a freshwater pump here that's usually working, so refill your bottles if needed. Check out the fancy, hand-painted shelter signs and leave a little love note in the log book to the Carteret County Wildlife Club, who, with some help from the USFS, does an impressive job of maintaining this coastal hiking treasure. Rest a moment at the shelter and then return by the same route.

Directions From Flanners Beach Campground, turn left onto US 70 East for 6.9 miles. Turn left onto Fontana Blvd., then keep left to stay on Fontana Blvd./NC 101 East for 5.2 miles. Turn left on NC 306 North for 3.3 miles, then turn left onto Pine Cliff Road. The Picnic Area is 0.5 mile down Pine Cliff Road.

Cedar Point Tideland Trail *1.4-mile loop, 45 minutes–1 hour, easy, marshland, maritime forest, boardwalk overlooks, interpretive signs, views of White Oak River*

■ Cedar Point Tideland Trail is a walk over the marsh.

You could probably get away with doing this walk in a pair of comfortable flip-flops. It's easy but worth a stroll. The trail starts near the bathrooms in the parking area for the Cedar Point Campground boat launch. Veer left to take the "long" option, unless you're really short on time; in which case, head right for a 0.6-mile mini-loop.

Interpretive signs, some a little faded, line the path, helping to solve mysteries like why fiddler crabs leave piles of tiny sand balls all over the beach. The elevated boardwalks provide phenomenal wildlife viewing along the White Oak River, which contains ospreys, herons, white-tailed hawks, and kayakers meandering along the paddle trail. (Hey, paddlers can get pretty wild.)

An unnoticeable elevation change of mere inches changes the landscape into a coastal forest, where the less salty environment allows red maple, sweetgum, white and red oak, longleaf pine, loblolly pine, and yellow poplar trees to thrive. These trees offer some welcome shade for the last section of your "hike," so take your time, watch the crabs scurry, and soak in this unique coastal ecosystem.

■ Wildlife-watching on Cedar Point Tideland Trail

> *Directions* From Flanners Beach Campground, take US 70 East for 27.6 miles; along the way it becomes Lake Road, 9 Mile Road, and NC 24 West. Follow VFW Road to Croatan Forest Road for 1.3 miles to the campground.

PADDLING ⊗

White Oak River *5.5-mile point-to-point, out-and-back option, put in at Dixon Field Landing*

The White Oak River is a blackwater treasure that runs for 48 miles from the Hofmann Forest, just northwest of the Croatan National Forest, to the Atlantic Ocean near Swansboro. This is a great trip if you want to get off the beaten path but not leave behind the convenience of an easy-to-find and well-maintained put-in with (primitive) restrooms.

■ Blackwater on the White Oak River

You'll paddle through blackwater swamp with ample tree canopy to protect you from wind and harsh sun. Watch for the patches of wildflowers that line the banks in the warmer months. You might spot beavers—or, at least, beaver dams—and alligators lurking in the dark, tannin-rich water.

Between the gator population and the swampland muck, don't plan on getting out of your boat (reason number 18 why we love having a bathroom at the put-in).

Put in at the gravel boat launch at Dixon Field Landing and head left to travel downriver, although the current moves slowly enough to make it easy to maneuver down- or upriver. There are a few places to venture off the main paddle trail, but these short side trips either dead-end or meet up with the main part of the river, so you'll stay on track. This is a good beginner paddle: the current is slow, the river never too tight or twisty, and the scenery superb. Unless it recently stormed, you should be able to paddle your boat carefully around any blowdowns. If you have two cars or arrange a shuttle, you can do an easy 5.5-mile paddle to the public boat launch at Haywood Landing or continue to Long Point Landing for an 8.8-mile trip. White Oak Campground offers a shuttle service some weekends; call for availability. No shuttle? No problem—it's just as easy to paddle back upstream. You can turn around whenever you're ready.

Directions to put-in From Flanners Beach Campground, turn right onto US 70 for 0.3 mile. Turn left onto Catfish Lake Road for 15.6 miles, then turn left onto NC 58 South. After 1.6 miles, turn right onto County Road 1102, and then right onto Dixon Field Road. Watch for the brown boat launch signs.

Directions to takeout From Dixon Field Landing, turn right onto County Road 1102 for 0.5 mile, then turn right onto NC 58 South for 2.8 miles. Make an immediate right on FR 120, then right onto FR 146.

Bear Island *5.2-mile out-and-back, marsh and sound paddling, put in at Hammocks Beach State Park*

Paddling to the undeveloped, 980-acre Bear Island is a popular excursion. However, once you leave the bustle of the Intracoastal Waterway and slip into the maze of marshland, you'll forget there's anyone else around. Well, other than the herons and ospreys . . . and the egrets . . . wait, is that a bottlenose dolphin? On a warm, sunny day, the rich green of the marsh grass, the sparkling reflection of the sun on the blue-gray water, and the seemingly never-ending expanse of sky will make you wish you were a painter, if you're not already. (We're better at kayaking than painting, though, so we'll stick to paddling with a camera handy.)

■ Kayak launch at Hammocks Beach State Park

Grab a map from the visitor center and start your picture-perfect paddle at the boat launch, designed with kayakers in mind. The paddle trail to Bear Island is marked with orange-and-white posts that are faded and occasionally difficult to spot; keep scanning as you paddle so you don't miss one. Head left from the boat launch, and—when it's safe to do so—head straight across the Intracoastal Waterway, which can get busy with motorized boat traffic on weekends. Veer to the right, scan for the orange-and-white posts, and slip into the quiet of the marsh. From this point, navigation is straightforward as you follow a tidal creek while it weaves through the tall marsh grass. At low tide, be prepared to portage through ankle-deep water. (In warm weather, it's kind of fun to get your toes in the sand.)

As you get close, Bear Island's mountainous dunes, lined with sea oats, seaside goldenrod, and American beach grass, loom before you. (Don't worry if you can't identify all of your coastal grasses; we're still working on that too.) When Bear Island is directly in front of you, turn left, hug the shore, and watch for a sandy patch of beach near campsite 14. (There's primitive, boat-in camping on Bear Island.) We like to stop at this little spot and explore the island. There are no official trails, but there are plenty of sandy footpaths to follow. May–August, humans aren't the only visitors to Bear Island: loggerhead sea turtles nest on its beaches too. Volunteers and park rangers monitor turtle activity through the summer.

■ Bear Island paddle campsite

If it's possible, paddle out at high tide, enjoy several hours exploring Bear Island, and return on the incoming high tide. Another option is put in during the middle of the outgoing high tide, then wait a short while at Bear Island before you paddle back with the tide. If you can't avoid a low tide launch, bear right at Cow Channel and head toward the ferry dock, where you can follow the ferry route (which, for obvious reasons, is much deeper). To make sure you return before the park closes, check the park schedule before you put in. If you're a beginner paddler or don't have a boat, Hidden Coast Adventure (910-612-3297, paddlenc.org) is commissioned by the park to offer kayak, canoe, and SUP rentals and tours; find them near the boat launch. We recommend this trip to paddlers with the experience and stamina to paddle against wind and tides. If you're short on either, don't despair: the park operates a ferry to the island April–October. Check ncparks.gov/hammocks-beach-state-park for more information.

Directions to put-in From Flanners Beach Campground, turn left onto US 70 East for 5.8 miles. Follow Lake Road and 9 Mile Road to NC 24 West for 13.1 miles, then turn right onto NC 24 West. After 12.1 miles, turn left onto Old Hammocks Road, then left again onto Hammocks Beach Road. Turn right into the park.

Cedar Point Campground Canoe Trail
2 miles, salt marsh, paddle around the Tideland Trail, put in at Cedar Point Campground Boat Launch

Start of the Cedar Point Canoe Trail

Think of this paddle as the wet version of the Cedar Point Tideland hiking trail; in fact, doing both loops would make for a nice paddle/hike mini-duathlon. It's also a beautiful spot to soak in a sunset from the White Oak River, especially if you're camping at Cedar Point Campground. It's ideal for a SUP trip, as the path is protected from the wind, although you might have to duck under some of the footbridges.

Put in at the Cedar Point Campground boat launch and look for the first yellow trail marker on the right. Continue to bear right around the point. You'll soon paddle under the first of three boardwalks, where hikers will probably be wildlife watching. You'll undoubtedly spot a few great blue herons and snowy egrets, but the beauty of a short and easy paddle is being able to take your time and really scope out some harder-to-spot wildlife finds. The wild-haired, long-beaked belted kingfisher hangs out around here, and you'll recognize the white-bellied tufted titmouse by the little puff on the top of its head. A few more for your scavenger hunt: the green anole, a medium-size lizard that can change colors from brown to green, and crabs of all varieties (fiddler, mud, and blue).

The Cedar Point Canoe Trail is short but wildly scenic.

After passing under the third bridge, head left, keeping close to the marsh and forest. Paddle a short stretch of open water before meeting up with the path you started on. (This route is more of a balloon than a circular loop.) Veer left around the point this time and return to the boat launch for a short but satisfying 2-mile paddle.

Directions to put-in See directions to Cedar Point Campground.

Stand Up Outfitters

White Oak River Campground
7660 New Bern Hwy., Maysville; 910-743-3051; whiteoakrivercampground.com

Kayak and canoe rentals, guided trips, shuttle services. Reservations are required, so call or email ahead to check on availability.

Stand Up Outfitters *244 Craven St., New Bern; 252-638-3000; standupoutfitters.com*

SUP rentals with delivery, classes, and sales. Great stop for paddle info and friendly service.

MAPS

Croatan National Forest U.S. Forest Service's *Croatan National Forest*. Available for purchase online at nationalforestmapstore.com. Overview maps of the Croatan National Forest and Neusiock Trail are both available at www.fs.usda.gov.

RAINY DAY

North Carolina History Center at Tryon Palace *529 South Front St., New Bern; 800-767-1560; tryonpalace.org*

There's a lot going on at this historic site, but the North Carolina History Center is hands-down the coolest part of Tryon Palace. The Pepsi Family Center transports you into a village from 1835 and offers lots of hands-on fun, and you'll even get a taste of the great outdoors as you meander through the "forest" in the Regional History Museum.

You can tour the rest of the palace too, but the History Center is more our cup of cocoa. Galleries pass: $12/adult, $6/child grades 1–12.

FOOD AND DRINK 🥤

Savage's *303 Metcalf St., New Bern; 252-672-0103*

Intimate, down-to-earth, family-run pizza joint with so many specialty pizzas it's hard to choose. We say get the Greek Vegetarian loaded (really, they don't skimp on toppings) with spinach, Kalamata olives, and tomatoes.

Brütopia *1201 US 70, New Bern; 252-631-5142; brutopiabeer.com*

Ask where to get a beer around New Bern and you'll end up here. Friendly, cool, and comfortable with 8–10 carefully curated beers on tap. Six-packs, growlers, and wine available too.

Brewery 99 *417F Broad St., New Bern; 252-259-6393*

Two things you need to know: 1) The brewery is located in a rather nondescript building that's hidden from the street by another rather nondescript building. 2) If you leave without talking to Pete, you're missing out on half the experience. The other half, of course, being the delicious and unique brews.

Trent River Coffee Company *208 Craven St., New Bern; 252-514-2030*

It's worth a stop for more than a good cup of coffee and the brick-wall, classic-coffee-shop atmosphere. The Twin Rivers Paddle Club (twinriverspaddleclub .org) meets here on some Saturdays for its Coffee Paddles; trip locations are determined over a cup of coffee, of course. They make all our coffee shop dreams come true by allowing dogs too.

GEAR AND RESUPPLY 🛒

Head either direction on US 70 from Flanners Beach Campground and you'll find gas stations within a few miles. There's also a Food Lion 10 miles north on US 70 in New Bern and a Walmart 5 miles south in Havelock.

Surf, Wind and Fire *230 Middle St., New Bern; 252-288-5823; surfwindandfire.com*

Limited selection of outdoor gear, including backpacks, tents, sleeping pads, and some paddling gear. And clothes. Lots of clothes.

The Four C's *250 Middle St., New Bern; 252-636-3285; thefourcs.com*

Outdoor gifts and clothing. Fun gifts downstairs, outdoor gear upstairs.

■ Beware of the bears in New Bern.

Beautiful views abound in Linville Gorge.

LINVILLE GORGE

There's no shortage of places claiming to be The Grand Canyon of the East, but we think Linville Gorge is the real deal. Bask in 360-degree views of the Blue Ridge from the top of the Chimneys. Descend 1,400 feet to the Linville River and stand in the cool shadows of sheer cliff walls and massive old-growth trees. This is one of our most challenging and primitive weekend adventures. The terrain is formidable, the navigation difficult, and campground amenities— and cell service—are nonexistent in the wilderness area. But if you're ready to trade crowds and your digital tether for a test of your physical prowess in some of the most spectacular terrain in North Carolina, this is your trip.

Areas included: Blue Ridge Parkway, Brown Mountain, Chimneys, Linville Caverns, Linville Gorge Wilderness Area, Linville River, Shortoff Mountain, Table Rock Mountain

Adventures: Camping, hiking, river swimming, climbing, cavern-exploring, paranormal activity

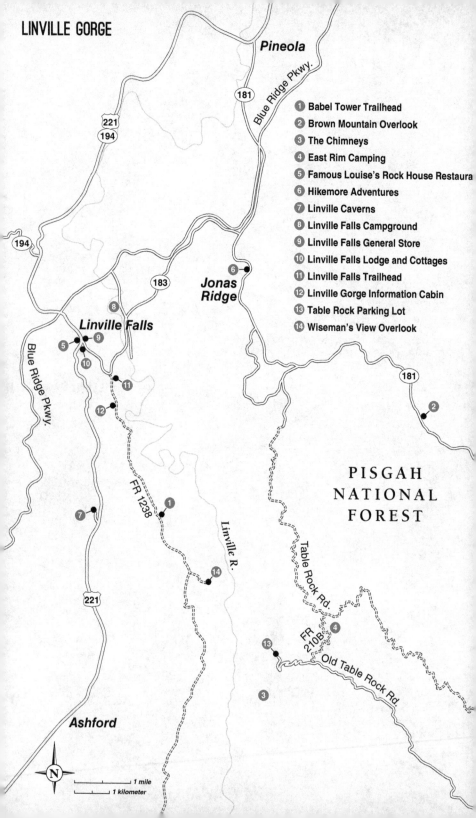

LINVILLE GORGE

Pineola

Jonas Ridge

Linville Falls

Ashford

PISGAH NATIONAL FOREST

1. Babel Tower Trailhead
2. Brown Mountain Overlook
3. The Chimneys
4. East Rim Camping
5. Famous Louise's Rock House Restaura
6. Hikemore Adventures
7. Linville Caverns
8. Linville Falls Campground
9. Linville Falls General Store
10. Linville Falls Lodge and Cottages
11. Linville Falls Trailhead
12. Linville Gorge Information Cabin
13. Table Rock Parking Lot
14. Wiseman's View Overlook

Blue Ridge Pkwy.

Blue Ridge Pkwy.

FR 1238

Linville R.

Table Rock Rd.

FR 210B

Old Table Rock Rd

N

1 mile
1 kilometer

LODGING

TOP PICK

PRIMITIVE CAR CAMPING ON THE EAST RIM *Primitive sites located along FS 210 and 210B on the east rim of the gorge; first come, first served; free; not maintained; no amenities*

As you slowly bump along the rough gravel of FS 210, you'll find numerous places to camp along the side of the road, especially near the Spence Ridge and Hawksbill Trailheads. These are perfectly acceptable primitive campsites as long as you keep your gear off the trails, but our favorite east rim sites are located 1–2 miles from the Table Rock parking lot. After you pass the Outward Bound School driveway on the right, start looking for openings in the forest. You'll find at least three great camping areas on the left between here and the junction with Old Table Rock Road. Camping permits are not required here, as this is not part of the designated Linville Gorge Wilderness Area.

■ Table for two at a Linville Gorge primitive campsite

If you want to camp even closer to the Table Rock area, have secured a permit, and don't mind a short walk to your car and lots of company, there are primitive campsites located about 0.1 mile from the Table Rock parking area, just past the picnic area. (*Note:* The paved road to the Table Rock parking lot is closed January–March.) Camping is not permitted in the picnic area, although you will likely see tents here. Show respect for the wilderness and don't camp illegally! You'll also have access to a pit toilet. Be sure to plan ahead. Unlike the roadside sites on FS 210, camping in the Linville Gorge Wilderness Area requires a free permit on weekends and holidays May–October, and only 50 permits are issued each weekend. Group size is limited to 10 and you can only reserve one weekend permit per month for up to three days and two nights. Call the Grandfather Ranger District at 828-652-2144 to reserve a permit, or visit the Linville Gorge Information Cabin (516 Old NC 105, Marion), where 15 walk-in permits are made available each Friday at 10 a.m. Find additional info at www.fs.usda.gov/recarea/nfsnc/null/recarea/?recid=48974&actid=37.

If you're used to setting up your tent in developed campgrounds, keep in mind that primitive camping in the gorge is a very different experience. The sites aren't numbered or maintained and offer little more than a small, cleared space where you can park your car on the side of the road and find a nook for your tent. You won't have running water, bathrooms, tent pads, or picnic tables, although some sites have camper-created fire rings. Keep in mind that you will need to bring all your drinking, cooking, and wash water with you when camping at higher elevations, as there are very few seasonal springs and seeps in the area.

Directions From the town of Linville Falls, take NC 183 South at its junction with US 221. After 4.5 miles, turn right onto NC 181 South and follow it 3 miles. Turn left onto Ginger Cake Road. At 0.3 mile, bear left onto FS 210 (Table Rock Road). Take FS 210 for 5.4 miles, and then turn right onto FS 210B. Primitive campsites are located along FS 210 and 210B. To get to the Table Rock parking lot, follow FS 210B for 1.3 miles from its intersection with FS 210 and turn right onto Old Table Rock Road (paved). The parking lot is 1.4 miles from here.

Note that the gravel road driving in this area is manageable by most vehicles, but the steep grade and deep potholes make the drive somewhat treacherous and extremely slow-going. Four-wheel drive is necessary in inclement weather.

View from the Chimneys

Here are a few tips for a successful trip:

Practice Leave No Trace principles. Take all trash with you, camp and travel on durable surfaces (don't create new tent or campfire areas), and be potty-prepared. When nature calls, use a small shovel or sturdy stick to dig a cathole 6–8 inches deep and at least 200 feet from camp and water sources. Cover and disguise your cathole when your duty is done, and for the love of all things adventure, never, never, NEVER leave your toilet paper on the ground.

Bring a smaller-than-usual tent or a hammock to increase your chances of finding a suitable camp-site. Some sites are on the small side.

Pack plenty of water. Think hard about what you'll need for drinking and cleaning. Adventures here are strenuous, so plan on two gallons of drinking water per person per day.

For food preparation, bring cooking gear you can use on the ground (think small backpacking-style stoves), the back of your car, or a packable table.

Keep all food, toiletries, and other smell-ables locked in your car when not using them to discourage animals from visiting your site. Keeping valuables on your person or locked in your car is also a good practice.

BACKUP BASE CAMP

Linville Falls Campground *Blue Ridge Parkway milepost 316.4; 828-765-7818; recreation.gov. $19/night, open April–October, 66 sites, reservations accepted for some sites, picnic table, fire ring, tent pad, flush toilets, shared water*

While you'll have to drive a bit more to access some of the gorge's adventures, especially those on the east rim, camping on the Blue Ridge Parkway is never a bad option. This is also a good choice if you prefer a more traditional camp-ground experience. Try to snag a riverside site in the A loop, if you can. Reserva-tions are recommended, but some sites are available on a first-come, first-served basis, so you might get lucky.

INDOOR LODGING

Linville Falls Lodge and Cottages *Address for GPS use: 8890 NC 183, Newland; 800-634-4421; linvillefallslodge.com. $95–$280/night, Wi-Fi, queen and king beds, lodge rooms and 1- and 2-bedroom cottages, outdoor grills, breakfast included*

Located in the Linville Falls community, the lodge is only minutes from the Linville Gorge Wilderness Area. The Lodge is not four-star luxury, but the property is beautiful, the lodge is cozily charming, and the service is top-notch. Rooms are small, but clean and well appointed, and you can enjoy a well-earned beer or cocktail on the restaurant's deck at the end of the day. If you're bringing a group, the cottages or Manor House both provide a great space to relax and rehash post-adventure.

HIKING

■ Linville Gorge and River

If you're trying to maximize adventure time and/or you're not a fan of the rough gravel road driving that you can't avoid in the Linville Gorge, note that the first two hikes are closer to the primitive camping on the east rim (FS 210), while the last two hikes are more convenient to the Linville Falls Campground. Keep in mind that trails inside a wilderness area are not signed or regularly maintained by the U.S. Forest Service.

Table Rock to Linville River *7-plus-mile out-and-back, 4–7 hours, strenuous, Linville River, swimming holes, views, backcountry camping opportunities*

Want a hike with wild river crossings, cool gorge coves, and steep, rugged climbs and descents? Well, you've got it. This hike starts at the Table Rock picnic area and leads hikers into the heart of the Linville Gorge. At the time of this writing, crossing the river required hikers to rock-hop or ford the river. The Linville River can rise quickly after a heavy rainstorm, so crossing the river safely is not always possible.

Start at the Table Rock parking area and head north on the Mountains-to-Sea Trail toward Table Rock (to the right of the information kiosk). After approximately 0.25 mile, turn left onto the unsigned junction with Little Table Rock Trail, heading up and over a small rise, and then continue right at a northwest-facing abutment of Table Rock Mountain. Head steeply downhill for 1 mile, where you'll cross two small creeks and pass several campsites.

At the well-used, widespread camping area at mile 1.25, take a hard right turn where the trail follows an old, rocky road grade uphill to its junction with the usually signed Spence Ridge Trail. Turn left to travel downhill on Spence Ridge and continue your descent for another mile into the gorge.

At the river, you'll find either a washed-out or newly repaired bridge—the U.S. Forest Service has not announced when, or if, the bridge will be replaced—and your river crossing. At low to moderate water levels, you should be able to cross downstream of the old bridge and stay mostly dry by carefully moving from boulder to boulder. Be ready to swim by unfastening your pack straps, in case you need to squirm out of them quickly.

Linville River

If the river here is impassible, enjoy some time at the river and return the way you came for a respectable 6 miles. If you choose to continue, cross the river and turn left onto the Linville Gorge Trail and follow its meandering path downstream. The trail is relatively flat along this stretch, but littered with rock gardens, root systems, and downfall, so tighten your bootlaces and hike carefully. At mile 3.5, you will reach a signed junction with the Conley Cove Trail on the right. This is the official turnaround point for this hike, and makes a great lunch stop where you can cool off in the river and enjoy views of the towering gorge walls. You are welcome to press on along the Linville River Trail for more scenery and rock scrambling, but remember that you have to retrace your steps. To return, hike upstream, cross the river at the "bridge," and head back the way you came.

Directions Follow directions to the Table Rock parking lot on page 94.

The Chimneys *2–4 miles (depending on turnaround point), out-and-back, 1–3 hours, moderate, 360-degree views, large cliffs*

This short trek makes a spectacular sunset or sunrise hike, and by going early or late you'll avoid the inevitable midday crowds. This hike isn't particularly long, but be prepared to do some hand-over-foot rock scrambling up to the Chimneys to claim the best views.

The Chimneys

Head south on the Mountains-to-Sea Trail (MST) from the Table Rock parking area, past the picnic area. No need to hurry—enjoy the 360-degree views along the ridgeline and watch your footing, as the trail drops steeply away on either side of the ridge. At mile 0.75 you'll arrive at the Chimneys, whose cliff faces rise close to the trail on your left. You can scramble

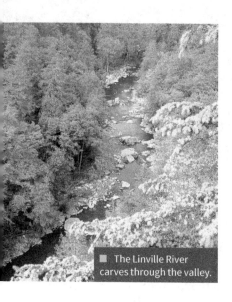

The Linville River carves through the valley.

up gullies between the faces to access the clifftops and take in the views ordinarily reserved for climbers. Continue south on the MST, down the top of the ridge, and turn left, where the trail opens up to views of Table Rock, the east side of the Chimneys, and the Piedmont to the southeast.

If you're craving a longer hike, you can continue rather steeply down the trail toward Chimney Gap at mile 1.8 through a fire-damaged landscape that offers even more views. Chimney Gap makes a good rest stop before you head back the way you came on the MST. Soak in the views from the other direction before you return to your car or camp.

Directions Follow directions to the Table Rock parking lot on page 94.

WANT TO DO SOME LOW-MILEAGE PEAK BAGGING?

Start at the Table Rock Trail, located to the right of the kiosk in the Table Rock parking lot. At 0.3 and 0.5 miles, stay right where side trails enter from the left. You'll reach the summit in a mile.

Babel Tower–Linville River Loop *3-mile loop, 2–3 hours, strenuous, Linville River, Babel Tower, views, swimming holes*

This hike is a challenging but manageable route that takes you from rim to river. Be sure to send a telepathic thank-you to the trail builders for the switchbacks that make this trek a little gentler than other Linville hikes!

From the Babel Tower Trailhead, hike north, heading down the ridge toward Babel Tower, a 70-foot granite cliff with views of Table Rock and Hawksbill. At the junction with the Linville Gorge Trail at 1.2 miles, turn right and follow the switchbacks downhill to the river.

You'll have to strategically maneuver yourself over large boulders and slippery roots, so take it easy and don't let the siren call of the rushing river lure you into an unsafe pace! At the bottom, you'll find deep pools that practically beg

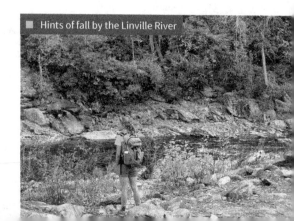

Hints of fall by the Linville River

you to take a swim, sandy banks ideal for a lunch stop, and truck-size boulders that you can carefully scale and explore. At this point, you can turn around and return the way you came or continue exploring by scrambling downstream along the Linville Gorge Trail. Just remember that hiking out of the gorge is a strenuous endeavor, so save some leg power for the return trip.

> **Directions** From the town of Linville Falls, take NC 183 south for 0.8 mile and turn right onto Kistler Memorial Highway (Old NC 105). Just over a mile up this rough gravel road (past the Linville Gorge Information Cabin), you'll find the Babel Tower Trailhead on the left.

Linville Falls Overlooks

Starting from the Linville Falls Campground/Visitor Center, Blue Ridge Parkway Milepost 316.4:
2-mile out-and-back, 1–2 hours, easy–moderate, views of Linville Falls and Gorge, three overlooks

Linville Falls

If you're camping at the Linville Falls Campground, this is the most convenient trailhead for a hike to Linville Falls, one of the most photographed views in North Carolina.

Cross the bridge over the Linville River near the Visitor Center and begin your hike on the Linville Falls Trail. Around 0.5 mile, turn left onto a spur trail to get your first taste of the falls at the Upper Falls overlook.

Ready for more? It only gets bigger and better from here! Continue briefly on the Linville Falls Trail, then turn left down steep steps to the Chimney View overlook, where you'll find a dramatic view of both the upper and lower falls. Get your classic Linville Falls shot here.

Return to the trail and continue on to Erwin's View, which offers several vantage points to take in a panoramic view of the falls and the gorge. Fun fact: at 90 feet, the falls are powerfully majestic, but they were 60 feet taller before a flood rerouted the river more than a hundred years ago. Soak in the views, and then return the way you came.

Starting from the Linville Gorge Wilderness Area, Kistler Memorial Hwy.:
2-mile out-and-back, easy–moderate

If you're camping on the east rim, this trailhead is a bit closer than the one at the Linville Falls Campground and it offers a chance to check out the gorge's west rim, where the Information Cabin is located. As you head toward the town of Linville Falls on NC 183, turn left onto the unpaved Kistler Memorial Highway (Old NC 105). Shortly after the turn, park at the lot on the left. The trail is located on the far right side of the parking lot. Follow the trail downhill and, at 0.4 mile, head left to reach the Upper Falls overlook, or stay right to reach the Chimney View and Erwin's View overlooks. Return along the same route.

CLIMBING

Linville is known for its steep, exposed gorge walls, which makes for excellent climbing adventures. There are several distinct climbing areas in the gorge, mostly located on the east rim, with opportunities ranging from bouldering and easy top-roping to multi-pitch trad routes that run from 5.4–5.12.

■ Top-roping at the Chimneys

The Chimneys *Single-pitch top-rope climbing, 5.4–5.9, best in fall, winter, and spring*

The Chimneys are a family-friendly area with numerous top-rope routes ranging from 5.4–5.9, with natural and bolted anchors. From the Table Rock picnic area, hike south on the Mountains-to-Sea Trail for 0.75 mile, up and over a rocky outcrop; you'll end up to the right of the Chimneys. There are two main cliff faces that share a steep gully access to the clifftop, where you can use a combination of bolt anchors set by the North Carolina Outward Bound School and natural anchors. Some routes have double bolts, while others have very large, stout single eye bolts cemented into the rock. Always use at least two equalized anchor points.

Table Rock *Single-pitch and multi-pitch climbing; 5.5–5.12; best in spring, summer, and fall*

Table Rock has good routes for newer trad climbers and hard-core, experienced dirtbags alike. Nearly every route requires at least some trad gear, though some are bolted at belay points. For this and other climbing areas in Linville, we highly recommend Yon Lambert and Harrison Shull's *Selected Climbs in North Carolina*.

■ Table Rock

The cliff faces on Table Rock generally point east and north, so even in hot summer months, you won't bake out on the rock. The climbing area is divided into three large sections: the South End, East Face, and North End. The East Face offers climbers the most routes. For adventurers new to trad, we recommend Peek-a-Boo (5.5) on the East Face due to its relatively moderate difficulty and the option to either rappel down from the top of the second pitch (two rappels) or take an easy (5.4) low-angle line up to "lightning ledge" and walk off. Another excellent climb on the East Face is Blood, Sweat, and Tears (5.7), a single-pitch lead that tops out on a ledge—at which point you'll use a tree and sling to rappel back to the ground.

Directions Head north on the MST from the Table Rock parking lot for 0.5 mile, and then turn right onto the access trail for the climbing areas. You'll pass a trail on the left that leads to the South End. Continue straight for the East Face and North End.

BONUS PICK: AMPHITHEATER CLASSICS

Numerous climbing areas are nicknamed the Amphitheater, but Linville's version is particularly spectacular. Exposed and steep, this area to the south and west of the Chimneys and the North Carolina Wall offers climbable multi-pitch trad routes in a less-traveled part of the gorge. You'll find several single-pitch options to the left of the Amphitheater's gully that offer a great warm-up for the day.

The Mummy (5.5, three pitches) and Daddy (5.6, five pitches) are popular routes, with lots of opportunities for placing protection. Both routes are located on the large, shark-fin shaped tower on the right (south) side of the Amphitheater. The Mummy starts on the left side of the tower and follows a long vertical crack to an arête, then finishes with a low-angle scramble to the top. The Daddy starts on the right side of this tower, stair-stepping several angled ledges as the route gradually moves right across the face. It joins with a broad ledge and traverses left to another series of vertical cracks and ledges aiming almost directly for the top.

■ Matt ties a Prusick knot at the base of the Chimneys.

Directions Follow directions to the Chimneys, then head south on the MST. Take the third side trail on the right (the first two lead to the Chockstone Chimney and North Carolina Wall). At the bottom of the hill, at a large, flat rock, stay left and continue around the gorge rim. The north side of the Amphitheater will be behind you and then to your right as you hike over the top of Reggae Buttress. Head down a steep gully to the top of the Mummy Buttress. Another gully to the right side of the buttress (looking downhill) will bring you to the bottom of the cliff. The total hike from the Table Rock parking area is under 2 miles, but accessing the bottom of the Amphitheater is a strenuous scramble in both directions.

CLIMBING NOTE

With the exception of the top-roping area at the Chimneys, we recommend that all climbing in Linville be undertaken with at least one of the following: the assistance of a climbing guidebook, experienced companions who know the area, or an AMGA instructor. The Mountain Project (mountainproject.com) has a forum where you can find information about falcon nesting closures, current conditions, and climbing beta.

Fox Mountain Guides *3228 Asheville Hwy., Pisgah Forest; 888-284-8433; foxmountainguides.com*

Instruction and guiding for all levels of climbers, including beginners.

Granite Arches Climbing Guides *423-413-1432, granitearches.com*

Formal instruction for skill enhancement and guiding services for beginner through advanced climbers.

PADDLING ⊗

With 6- to 7-mile stretches of nonstop Class IV–V+ rapids and stunning scenery, the Linville River is the crown jewel of Eastern rivers for expert paddlers. That said, we don't recommend a paddle trip on the Linville River as part of your weekend adventure because, well, we want you to make it to the next weekend.

OTHER ADVENTURES ⊕

Linville Caverns *19929 US 221 N., Marion; 800-419-0540; linvillecaverns.com*

Located inside of Humpback Mountain, North Carolina's only caverns offer a caving experience that kids and claustrophobics (you can opt out of exploring the cavern's tightest areas) can both enjoy. Take a 30-minute tour in this subterranean world and stroll on lighted paths among stalactites, stalagmites, and an underground stream swarming with speckled trout. It's always a cool 52°F and usually wet in the cave, so dress accordingly. Fee: $8/adult, $6/child, no strollers or kid-hauling backpacks allowed inside the caverns.

> **Directions** From the intersection of NC 183 and US 221 in the Linville Falls community, head southwest on US 221 for 3.2 miles.

Wiseman's View Overlook

NOCTURNAL ADVENTURES

Brown Mountain Lights What have your weekend adventures been missing? Obviously, paranormal activity . . . or rumors of it. These mysterious, multicolored orbs of light appear to float haphazardly around Brown Mountain, blinking slowly like a giant mutant lightning bug. (If such a thing existed. We're not here to spread rumors.) There's no shortage of theories to explain the lights' origins—ghosts, extraterrestrials, gaseous activity, ball lightning, and human imagination, just to name a few—and indeed one of your authors was a BML skeptic before witnessing them firsthand. Whatever they are, they're worth rallying to see after a day of adventuring. Make the drive to check them out after it gets dark.

WHERE TO FIND THEM:

Brown Mountain Overlook 20 miles north of Morganton on NC 181, 1 mile south of the Barkhouse Picnic Area. It's a bit of a drive from the Linville Gorge, but still our favorite spot for BML sightings. Wide open views, informational signs, and no night hiking required.

GPS coordinates: N35° 56.525' W81° 50.513'

Wiseman's View Overlook From Linville Falls, take Kistler Memorial Highway (Old NC 105) 4 miles. Hike 0.2 mile to the viewing area.

GPS coordinates: N35° 54.232' W81° 54.286'

Table Rock BML sightings are less common here, but this is a closer option if you're camping on the east rim. Follow the directions for the Table Rock parking lot, bring a headlamp or flashlight, and hike carefully.

MAPS

Linville Gorge Wilderness Area U.S. Forest Service's *Linville Gorge Wilderness: Pisgah National Forest.* Available for purchase at the Linville Gorge Information Cabin on Kistler Memorial Highway or online.

Linville Gorge Community online maps Linvillegorge.net is an online community and message board that offers user-generated, downloadable GPS and PDF maps of every trail in the wilderness, along with useful information about current trail and river conditions. The forum is free to join, but membership is required to access maps and trail information.

> **MAP NOTE**
>
> National Geographic's *Linville Gorge and Mount Mitchell* map is a suitable area map to get you around the area by car, but it does not provide enough detail to serve as your primary hiking map.

FOOD AND DRINK 🍴

Famous Louise's Rock House Restaurant *23175 Linville Falls Hwy., Linville Falls; 828-765-2702*

Old-fashioned Southern comfort food and seafood, made just like your Southern grandma would do it. Whatever you order, you must have pie after your meal . . . or for your meal. One of your authors had her first piece of rhubarb pie after a flying-over-the-handlebars bike misadventure and was instantly cured—or close to it, at least.

GEAR AND RESUPPLY 🛒

Linville Falls General Store *8896 NC 183, Linville Falls; 828-765-1342*

Forget the fuel, flashlight, snacks, or even the camp stove? Even if you didn't, this store is so darn cute that you'll want to make a pit stop anyway. Basic groceries and camping supplies, gift-worthy souvenirs, and friendly service too.

Hikemore Adventures *9041 NC 181, Jonas Ridge; 828-595-4453; hikemoreadventures.com*

Check one more time; sure you didn't forget anything? This will be your last chance to pick up camping gear before heading onto the east rim, so stop by Hikemore's outpost for supplies, local information, or even to book a guided hiking or fly-fishing trip . . . wine and hammocks included.

Paddling the Alligator River

OUTER BANKS

We were a little intimidated by the idea of conquering the Outer Banks in one weekend, but we think we've got it down. Set up camp at Oregon Inlet Campground on Cape Hatteras National Seashore, where some of the best Outer Banks adventures are right outside your tent door. Paddle through marshland, maritime forests, or upland swamp. Bike past dunes and over bridges straight from your campsite. Hike nature trails crawling with wildlife and climb to the top of monumental sand dunes. Up for more? It only takes a few hours to get the hang of hang gliding at Jockey's Ridge State Park, and some of the best surfing on the East Coast can be found in this area. Oh . . . and the beach? It's just across the dunes from your campsite, so when you're adventured-out, grab your beach chair and relax. We have no doubt you've earned it!

Areas included: Alligator River National Wildlife Refuge, Jockey's Ridge State Park, Kill Devil Hills, Kitty Hawk, Kitty Hawk Woods, Nags Head, Oregon Inlet, Pea Island National Wildlife Refuge

Adventures: Camping, road biking, hiking, paddling, hang gliding, surfing

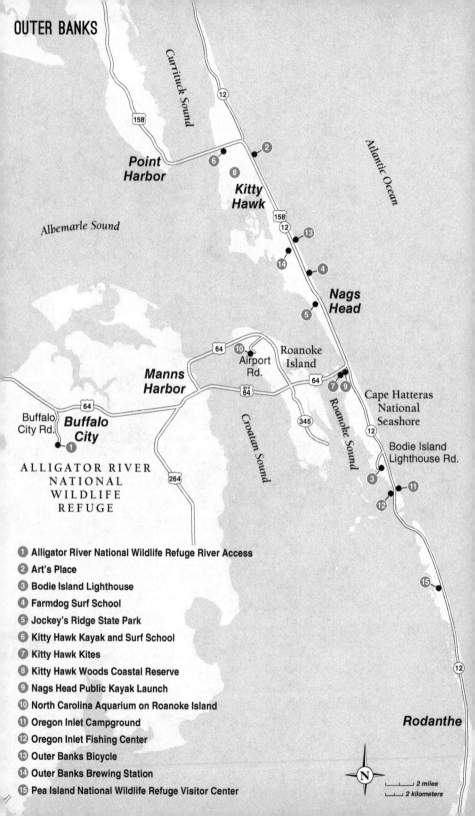

OUTER BANKS

1. Alligator River National Wildlife Refuge River Access
2. Art's Place
3. Bodie Island Lighthouse
4. Farmdog Surf School
5. Jockey's Ridge State Park
6. Kitty Hawk Kayak and Surf School
7. Kitty Hawk Kites
8. Kitty Hawk Woods Coastal Reserve
9. Nags Head Public Kayak Launch
10. North Carolina Aquarium on Roanoke Island
11. Oregon Inlet Campground
12. Oregon Inlet Fishing Center
13. Outer Banks Bicycle
14. Outer Banks Brewing Station
15. Pea Island National Wildlife Refuge Visitor Center

TOP PICK

OREGON INLET CAMPGROUND (NATIONAL PARK SERVICE) *12001 NC 12, Nags Head; 252-441-6246; nps.gov/caha/planyourvisit/campgrounds.htm. $28/night, open third Friday in April–first Monday after the last weekend in November, 120 sites, reservations accepted, picnic table, grill, flush toilets, central water, warm showers, wood fires not allowed. RVs can use the dump and water fill station at the Oregon Inlet Fishing Center, across from the campground.*

You'll meet especially happy campers at Oregon Inlet. And why shouldn't they be? For $28 a night, they've got their own piece of prime Outer Banks real estate. Not up for lounging at the beach all day? (Which, if you're reading this book, you're probably not.) There are tons of adventures within a 20-mile radius of the campground.

While every site is just a short stroll through the dunes to the beach, our favorite sites are in the B loop. Most of the sites from B5 to B15 are tucked against the dunes or tall bushes, providing a bit of wind protection. All these sites are grassy, so there will be slightly less sand in your tent. When the wind is blowing onshore, you'll hear more crashing waves than road traffic in these sites too. Tent campers share this part of the campground with RVs, but we still think it's preferable to the tent-only area, where sites are small, uneven, and sandy. The bathrooms and showers have been recently renovated and there are bottle-filling stations with cold water. If you're arriving after 7 p.m., call 252-441-6246 for registration information.

Keep in mind that beach camping is a different sort of beast. There are no trees, which means no shade, no place to hang a hammock or a tarp, and no privacy. When the wind is really blowing—which it often is—it can destroy tents and canopies. When the wind dies down, bugs invade. But don't put away your surfboard and sand toys yet. Here are a few beach camping survival tips:

- When it comes to tent stakes, go for quality and quantity. When you're staking out in sandy conditions, the longer the stakes the better. Stake out as many points as possible. If you haven't already, attach guylines to every loop on your tent fly, then stake out every line. It might look a little ridiculous, but not as ridiculous as chasing your tent as it flies like a kite through the campground.

- Generally, smaller, shorter tents do better than behemoth ones. That said, our six-person mansion survived our last beach camping adventure . . . but we did have it staked out at 14 points.

- Most sites at Oregon Inlet, besides those in the tent-only area, are covered in thick, luscious grass. (NPS, how do you do it?) However, if you do end up in a sandy site, you can keep your tent from turning into a sandbox. Put a small kiddie pool or shallow container of water next to your tent door to wash your feet before going inside. It helps to keep a small doormat or rug there too. Line the inside of your tent floor with a canvas drop cloth, which you can get cheaply at any hardware store, or a heavy sheet, and shake out as needed. Or, pick up one of those cute mini tent brooms—heck, you can just bring your broom from home if you have room in the car and a big tent to keep clean.

- Use screen houses and quick setup canopies with caution. Smart campers will use them for shade and bug protection when it's not too windy, and take them down when they leave camp. Coastal weather can change in an instant, and returning to your site to find a mangled heap of metal and nylon is no day at the beach.

Directions *From the west and south* Take US 64 East, through Roanoke Island, to Whalebone Junction in Nags Head. Just past the causeway, turn right onto NC 12 South, following signs for Cape Hatteras National Seashore. The campground is on your left in 8 miles.

From the north Take US 158 South to Nags Head and turn left onto NC 12 South, following signs for Cape Hatteras National Seashore. Oregon Inlet Campground is 8 miles south on the left.

■ The beach at Oregon Inlet Campground

BACKUP BASE CAMP

We don't recommend the handful of private campgrounds in this area, as they are mostly cramped RV parks. However, on our last trip over a peak-season weekend, there were still sites available at Oregon Inlet.

INDOOR LODGING

If for some crazy reason you want air-conditioning and hot showers, there are multitudes of hotel, bed-and-breakfast, and vacation-rental options. Outerbanks .org provides an easy-to-browse list of current lodging vacancies and rental recommendations.

ROAD BIKING

■ Kitty Hawk Woods

Road biking is pretty easy to DIY around here. Most of the section of NC 12 in the National Seashore offers decent riding, and you can do a satisfying out-and-back ride—your choice of distance—right from your tent door. Head south on NC 12 and it's 7 miles to the Pea Island Visitor Center and 16 miles to Beads & Beans OBX, a coffee shop with a great ocean view in Rodanthe. A few tips: NC 12 generally has good shoulders, but can get narrow in places, especially through Pea Island. Saturday mornings bring a lot of traffic, but start at first light and you won't face the brunt of it. And, while the terrain is pancake flat (except for the bridges), a steady headwind can work you as hard as a mountain climb. If you're going out with a tailwind, keep in mind that your return trip might be an epic workout!

Prefer a loop? Check out Outer Banks Bicycle's website, outerbanksbicycle .com, where you'll find several detailed ride descriptions with maps. Your best bet for an easy-to-navigate weekend loop is the 25-mile Morning Ride in Kitty Hawk, but there are other options too, including a fat-tire beach ride to Virginia. Stop by the shop at 203 South Virginia Dare Trail in Kill Devil Hills for friendly service, riding info, a huge gear selection, and rentals. For current biking information, or to meet up with other riders, check out the OBX Cycling Facebook page.

HIKING ●

Pea Island National Wildlife Refuge North Pond Wildlife Trail *1-mile out-and-back, 30–45 minutes, easy, turtle pond, marsh views, binocular spotting scopes, observation tower, interpretive signs*

Pea Island North Pond Trail

The Pea Island National Wildlife Refuge was established in 1938 as a protected habitat and breeding area for migratory birds. As the friendly visitor center volunteer reminded us, the refuge's primary purpose is to benefit wildlife—it's an added bonus that humans get to enjoy its pristine beaches and serene scenery.

The trail is open sunrise–sunset, so hike early morning or in the evening to maximize wildlife spotting. (Just don't forget your bug spray, especially in the summer, unless you also want to observe the local insect population.) This gravel path takes you over a stocked turtle pond and through a tunnel of live oak trees, and it ends at a double-decker observation tower overlooking North Pond and the marsh.

Take your time; there are interpretive signs lining the path and binoculars for wildlife viewing. You'll probably recognize the great blue heron, great egret, and brown pelican, but with 350 bird species in the refuge, you're likely to spot something new to you. The visitor center has knowledgeable volunteers, lots of free literature, interesting displays, cold drinks, bug spray, and a great guidebook selection.

Directions From Oregon Inlet Campground, turn left (south) on NC 12 for 6.9 miles.

Kitty Hawk Woods Coastal Reserve *8 miles of trails, easy, interpretive signs, maritime forest, swamp, marsh, covered bridge, bike path and off-road biking*

This place is a hidden gem. Though it was once slated to be part of a development, the state of North Carolina acquired most of the land through a conservation easement in the early 1990s. Now visitors can explore a rare maritime deciduous forest, maritime swamp forest, and marsh habitat without leaving the preserve. Enjoy coastal rarities, such as gently rolling terrain, freshwater ponds, and shade from dogwood, holly, and sassafras trees, as you hike or bike the trails (mountain bikes recommended).

It's hard to get lost here, as few trails are longer than a mile and you'll find signed trail junctions throughout the preserve. While some of the trails get overgrown in the summer, most are passable. We recommend starting

Kitty Hawk Woods covered bridge

at the Ridge Road trailhead to avoid sandy off-road driving and because there's a map posted at this trailhead. If you're up for a family bike ride, The Woods Road, which bisects the preserve, has a shady, paved bike path. Park at the David Paul Pruitt, Jr. Park, next to Dominion Power (5300 The Woods Road).

Directions From Oregon Inlet Campground, go 8 miles north on NC 12. Turn right onto US 158 for 12.2 miles. Turn left onto West Kitty Hawk Road for 2.7 miles, then turn right onto Ridge Road. The trailhead is at the end of the street.

Sandy Ridge Trail at Alligator River National Wildlife Refuge

Alligator River National Wildlife Refuge *1-mile out-and-back, 30–45 minutes, easy, creek views, boardwalk, interpretive signs*

This nature stroll is a great way to explore the refuge and stretch your legs on dry land after a paddle. The trail borders the paddle trail on Milltail Creek, passing through wetlands and marsh. Most of the trail is built on an elevated boardwalk, so your feet won't get swamped. The path is lined with interpretive signs, and if you travel slowly and quietly enough, you might spot an American alligator, wood duck, river otter, cockaded woodpecker, or prothonotary warbler, a striking yellow-bodied bird with gray wings. If walking slowly or speaking softly is a challenge, as it often is for the under-10 crowd or enthusiastic adventurers in general, enjoy the plant life instead. Watch for the carnivorous pitcher plant. Pause at the end of the trail and listen for wolves, and—if you're so inspired—try out your best wolf howl before returning the way you came.

Directions From Oregon Inlet Campground, head north on NC 12 for 8 miles. Turn left onto South Virginia Dare Trail, then left onto US 158 East. Continue straight onto US 64 West for 18.7 miles, then turn left onto Buffalo City Road for 2 miles.

PADDLING ⊗

Jean Guite Creek, Kitty Hawk Woods Coastal Reserve *4-plus miles, creek paddling with option to paddle in Kitty Hawk Bay, put in at Kitty Hawk Kayak*

■ Jean Guite Creek (photographed by Will Fisher/Flickr.com/CC BY-SA 2.0 [creativecommons.org/licenses/by-sa/2.0])

This out-and-back paddle through a maritime forest is the perfect trip for new or beginner paddlers. It's also one of the few bodies of water in the area that's protected from wind, so paddle here on especially blustery days. You won't always find much solitude on the creek, but if you head out early to mid-morning or in the evening, there will be fewer paddlers and more wildlife. Keep an eye out for white-tailed deer and raccoons on the land. In the water, look for river otters, turtles, and nutria, a web-footed river rat. Snakes (including the poisonous water moccasin) like it here too, so avoid getting out of your boat. And don't worry: snakes have no desire to get in your boat.

Paddle south from the boat launch through the blackwater, enjoying the shade of the cypress trees lining the banks. The route is a fairly straight shot, but there are small coves that are easy to explore without getting off-track. You'll also paddle under the only covered bridge in Eastern North Carolina. At mile 2, you'll reach the public boat launch, a good turnaround point for a 4-mile trip. Experienced paddlers can continue on to Kitty Hawk Bay, but it will be less protected from the elements and motorized boats. To reach Kitty Hawk Bay, stay to the right after passing Midgetts Pond. About 0.5 mile after the pond, turn left to explore the bay, then retrace your path.

> **Directions to put-in** From Oregon Inlet Campground, head north on NC 12 for 8.2 miles. Turn right onto US 158 West. In 16 miles, Kitty Hawk Kayak is on the left.

Alligator River National Wildlife Refuge *1.5-plus miles, creek and lake paddling, put in at Buffalo City Road Access*

There are plenty of adventures in the Outer Banks, but the Alligator River, home to red wolves, black bears, and yes, alligators, feels especially wild. You have to be a true adventurer to delve into this wild and mysterious 154,000-acre upland swamp. Don't worry: while the refuge isn't on the beaten path, the U.S. Department of Fish & Wildlife has done a great job ensuring you explore safely. There's plenty of roadside parking, maps, and portable restrooms at the boat launch, and the 13 miles of paddle trails have color-coded markers that make navigation easy. If you don't have your own boat, the department offers guided canoe trips, as do many local outfitters.

Alligator River Paddle

The refuge is open sunrise–sunset and we recommend getting your boat in the water as early as possible for maximum solitude. (At least from people—the bugs will keep you plenty company in the early morning hours, so bring bug repellent.) Or, paddle just before sunset to watch for black bears, which are surprisingly plentiful in this area. Just don't forget that the refuge closes at sunset. There's little shade out on the water, so avoid midday trips in warm weather.

At the boat launch grab a map, which shows four marked trails. The 1.5-mile red loop trail is a perfect beginner paddle, or do an out-and-back trip on any of the other trails. Turn right from the boat launch, heading under the low footbridge. To paddle the red loop—with a chance to add on additional mileage—turn left past the bridge to follow the blue and red trails. Continue left to stay on the red trail, which meanders through an old canal. The path is occasionally narrow and twisty; just paddle slowly. You might find a few overgrown sections, but a strong stroke will get you through. Eventually, the red trail joins the green trail. Here, you can turn left to finish the red trail loop, or, if you're up for a longer trip, turn right at the lake to return on the green trail. On our last trip, we paddled alongside cypress trees, swamp pine, turtles, copperhead snakes, alligators, frogs, and lizards. The first red wolf recovery program began here and, today, 50–75 of these critically endangered canids roam the five-county area in and around the refuge. Remember that all wildlife should be viewed at a respectful distance.

Directions See directions to Alligator River on page 114.

Marshes of Bodie Island, Roanoke Sound *3.5-plus miles, marsh and sound paddling, put in at the Nags Head Public Kayak Launch on US 158 (just east of Kitty Hawk Kites)*

This paddle starts in a sheltered part of the Roanoke Sound. Don't be intimidated by the roaring Jet Skis doing laps outside of Kitty Hawk Kites; it's easy to keep your distance and you'll soon trade the roar of engines for the calm quiet of the marsh.

Keep left and paddle south through the marsh, working your way around the east side of Headquarters Island. Our last paddle here had a pastoral feel to it; we kayaked past hunting blinds and towering marsh grasses that were reminiscent of a late-summer cornfield. Veer to the right through the marsh between Headquarters and Bells Islands. Directly ahead, you'll see a house on an unnamed island. With the house on your left, you can turn north around the west side of Headquarters Island toward your launch point for a 3.5-mile loop, or continue south around Bells Island to explore the green islands, as this area is known. The water can get shallow, but you can comfortably paddle just before or after low tide. Waterfowl hunting is popular during the fall hunting season, which usually only lasts a few weeks.

The calm waters of the sound are also an ideal spot for SUPs (at least, when the winds aren't raging). Kitty Hawk Kites, just on the other side of the parking

Paddle boarders appreciate the calm waters around Bodie Island.

lot, rents boards. This is also a prime location for an evening kayak. You don't have to paddle far to catch a brilliant sunset from the water and Kitty Hawk Kayak offers full moon and bioluminescence tours in the sound. Daytime paddling can get pretty toasty in the summer months, so you might prefer to paddle after dinner, anyway. The boat launch has plenty of parking, a small dock that's great for watching paddlers and wildlife, and a portable toilet.

> **Directions to put-in** From Oregon Inlet Campground, head north on NC 12 for 8 miles, then turn left onto US 158/64 toward Roanoke Island and Manteo. Look for the kayak put-in just past some bait shops on your left as you drive onto the causeway. If you pass Kitty Hawk Kites, you've gone too far.

Kitty Hawk Kayak *6150 N. Croatan Hwy., Kitty Hawk; 252-261-0145; khkss.com*

Kayak, SUP, surfboard, and bike rentals, guided trips and lessons. Private boats can put in at their launch in Kitty Hawk Woods for $5.

Kitty Hawk Kites *7517 S. Virginia Dare Trail, Nags Head; 252-441-4112; kittyhawk.com*

Kitty Hawk Kites has numerous locations and offers guided trips and rental gear for just about every outdoor adventure you can imagine.

MAPS

Alligator River National Wildlife Refuge Paddle and hiking trail map of the Milltail Creek area available at the parking area or online at www.fws.gov/south east/pubs/All_river_tearsheet.pdf.

Kitty Hawk Woods Area map posted at trailhead and available online at tinyurl .com/khwoods.

Marshes of Bodie Sound Printable NOAA charts of this part of the coast are available at charts.noaa.gov/BookletChart/12204_BookletChart.pdf.
> For map geeks, the USGS 7.5-minute quadrangle is *Roanoke Island NE*.

OTHER ADVENTURES +

HANG GLIDING AND SANDBOARDING
Jockey's Ridge State Park *Milepost 12 on US 158 Bypass; 252-441-7132; jockeysridgestatepark.com*

Even if hang gliding and sandboarding don't make your adventure weekend agenda, you'll still want to check out Jockey's Ridge. Take in 360-degree views from 80- to 100-foot-high "living dunes" that are constantly being shaped and moved by the wind. You won't be able to resist racing down these mountains of sand at least once—just don't forget your shoes, as the sand can get extremely hot.

Hang gliding over the dunes at Jockey's Ridge State Park

Ready to fly? Kitty Hawk Kites offers hang gliding lessons year-round; times vary. Want to add an even more obscure sport to your repertoire? Sandboarding (think snowboarding, but on sand) is allowed on the dunes. A permit is required (available in the visitor center) and boards with bindings are only allowed October–March. If you didn't think to bring your snowboard to the beach, Kitty Hawk Kites rents boards.

Hike the Tracks in the Sand Trail that runs through the park's lush maritime forest. The name is no tease: head out first thing in the morning and see what animals have left their footprints. The park is home to deer, red and gray fox, opossums, shorebirds, raccoons, and the six-lined racerunner, the fastest lizard in North America. The visitor center has some phenomenal hands-on displays that explore the park's geology, weather, and wildlife; this makes a great (and free) rainy day activity!

If you need to cool off after playing in the desertlike dunes, you can swim, kayak, or even windsurf (if you have the gear) on the calm waters of the Roanoke Sound, located in the southwest corner of the park.

SURFING

Where to surf in the Outer Banks? Well . . . it depends. While you'll usually find decent swell somewhere along the coast in this area, save your precious weekend minutes and visit obxsurfinfo.com and obxlivesurf.com to get up-to-date info on surf conditions. For both safety's and enjoyment's sake, we recommend that new surfers take a lesson. Check out Kitty Hawk Kayak and Farmdog Surf School (2500 S. Virginia Dare Trail, Nags Head; 252-255-2233; farmdogsurf school.com).

The waves at the campground's beach are usually good enough for beginner surfers who just want to practice getting up and staying up on the board (like us). Locals all agree that September–December is the best time of year for consistent swells without needing a wetsuit.

BEACH DRIVING

Has your four-wheel drive been asking to go to the beach too? Driving on the beach is allowed in designated areas, but plan ahead. You'll need to apply for a permit online at nps.gov or stop by the Bodie Island Lighthouse Visitor Center, just north of Oregon Inlet Campground. There's a list of required and recommended equipment on the NPS website, along with information on accessibility, closures, and so on. A seven-day permit is $50.

RAINY DAY 😷

North Carolina Aquarium on Roanoke Island *374 Airport Road, Manteo; 252-475-2300; ncaquariums.com*

Touch a stingray, observe feeding time, and explore the sea turtle center. Open water-certified scuba divers can even swim with the sharks, but everyone can enjoy observing the 285,000-gallon Graveyard of the Atlantic Exhibit from the dry side of the glass. Fee: $12.95/adult, $10.95/child. Open daily, 9 a.m.–5 p.m., except for Thanksgiving and Christmas.

FOOD AND DRINK 🍴

Outer Banks Brewing Station *600 S. Croatan Hwy., Kill Devil Hills; 252-449-2739; obbrewing.com*

It's never a bad time to visit the Outer Banks Brewing Station, the first wind-powered brewery in the United States. On nice days, you can play games or just kick back while enjoying a refreshing Lemongrass Wheat Ale outside as the kids run off excess energy at the playground. Or grab a seat at the bar and watch the magic of beer brewing through the large windows. Live music on weekends too.

Art's Place *4624 N. Virginia Dare Trail, Kitty Hawk; 252-261-3233; artsplaceobx.com*

"Locals welcome . . . tourists tolerated." Visiting adventurers, don't be intimidated: the service at this small, low-key restaurant is as good as their perfect food. We were revived after a day of nonstop adventure with their not-too-healthy veggie burgers, sweet potato fries, watermelon-basil coolers, and North Carolina beer. Art's is pretty small, so get there early for dinner to avoid a wait.

GEAR AND RESUPPLY 🛒

Head north from Oregon Inlet Campground on US 158 into Nags Head for grocery stores and just about anything else you might want. Just need the basics— ice, fuel, charcoal, long tent stakes, ice cream, or beer? (FYI, all of those are certified Adventure Weekend staples.) Hit up the Oregon Inlet Fishing Center, just across the street from the campground, open daily, 5 a.m.–7 p.m.

"SWEET JUMP AHEAD"

There's a lot of sweet riding to be done in the Raleigh area.

RALEIGH-RESEARCH TRIANGLE

The Raleigh area is bursting at the seams with outdoor fun—and passionate locals who are happy to help you find it. Every outfitter, bike shop, and trailhead we visited had adventurers offering to lend a hand, share advice, or, in one case, invite us to their house to shower. (Maybe it's time to reconsider our weekend hygiene?) They've got good reason to be excited about the outdoor opportunities here, where you'll find more rivers and lakes than you can shake a paddle at. There are miles and miles of hiking trails that might even fool you into thinking you're in the mountains. And no bike should be left behind—there's road and mountain biking for every rider, all within 30 minutes of your campsite.

Areas included: Eno River, Eno River State Park, Falls Lake Recreation Area, Jordan Lake, Lake Crabtree County Park, Neuse River, West Point on the Eno City Park, William B. Umstead State Park

Adventures: Camping, mountain and road biking, hiking, river and lake paddling

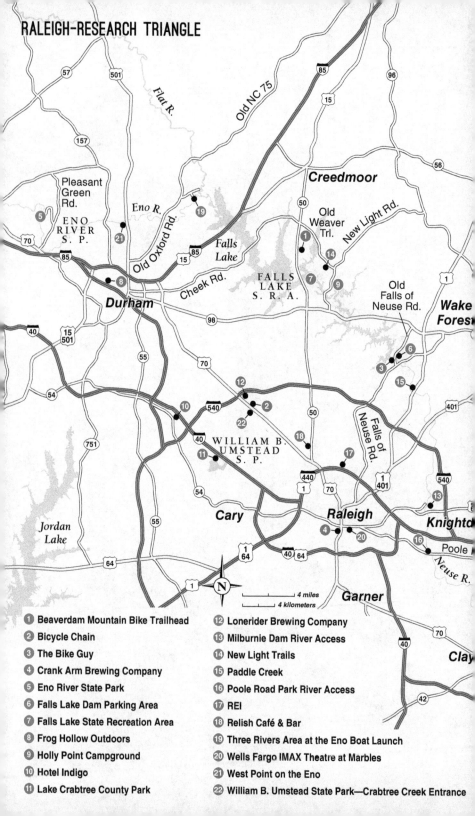

RALEIGH-RESEARCH TRIANGLE

Pleasant Green Rd.

ENO RIVER S. P.

Eno R.

Flat R.

Old NC 75

Creedmoor

Old Weaver Trl.

New Light Rd.

Falls Lake

Old Oxford Rd.

Cheek Rd.

FALLS LAKE S. R. A.

Old Falls of Neuse Rd.

Wake Fores

Durham

William B. Umstead S. P.

Falls of Neuse Rd.

Jordan Lake

Cary

Raleigh

Knightd

Poole

Neuse R.

Garner

Clay

4 miles
4 kilometers

N

1. Beaverdam Mountain Bike Trailhead
2. Bicycle Chain
3. The Bike Guy
4. Crank Arm Brewing Company
5. Eno River State Park
6. Falls Lake Dam Parking Area
7. Falls Lake State Recreation Area
8. Frog Hollow Outdoors
9. Holly Point Campground
10. Hotel Indigo
11. Lake Crabtree County Park
12. Lonerider Brewing Company
13. Milburnie Dam River Access
14. New Light Trails
15. Paddle Creek
16. Poole Road Park River Access
17. REI
18. Relish Café & Bar
19. Three Rivers Area at the Eno Boat Launch
20. Wells Fargo IMAX Theatre at Marbles
21. West Point on the Eno
22. William B. Umstead State Park—Crabtree Creek Entrance

LODGING

TOP PICK

WILLIAM B. UMSTEAD STATE PARK (NC STATE PARKS) *8801 Glenwood Ave., Raleigh; 919-571-4170; ncparks.gov/william-b-umstead-state-park. $15/night, open March 15–December 1, 28 sites, reservations accepted, picnic table, fire ring, tent pad, lantern hook, flush toilets, hot showers, central water*

Just a short trip from downtown Raleigh, this campground is a tent camper's dream. There are no electric or water hookups, and only a few sites are suitable for RVs. Almost all of the sites on the outside of the loop are spacious and back up into the woods. Sites 16 and 22 are especially spacious and private, but you'll do almost as well in sites 1–18 too. The tent pads, big enough for one large or two small tents, are raised, well graveled, and have substantial wooden borders.

While it was almost a full house over Labor Day weekend on our last trip, it's usually not hard to snag a site, even at the last minute. We'd say you'd completely forget that you're camping in North Carolina's capital, except that when you're only 7 miles from an international airport, the sound of air traffic does bring you back to reality. The plane noise subsides 10 p.m.–6 a.m., so you don't have to worry about not getting your beauty sleep. And while you won't write home about the bathhouse amenities, you'll have flush toilets and hot showers (what else do you need when you're camping?? There are great hands-on displays in the visitor center that are entertaining and informational for kids and adults alike. A word of warning: Before you leave home, check the park hours, which vary by season. When the gates are locked, there's no way to get in.

Directions to the Crabtree Creek Entrance From the south and the east On I-40 West, take Exit 301 for I-440 West/US 64 East. Follow I-440 West for 9.2 miles. Take Exit 7B for US 70/Glenwood Ave. Follow US 70/Glenwood Ave. for 5.8 miles, then turn left into the park.

From the north On I-85 South, take Exit 178 to US 70 East/Glenwood Ave. After 11 miles, turn right into the park.

From the west On I-40 East, take Exit 283 to merge onto I-540 East for 4.5 miles. Take Exit 4A for US 70 East. Merge onto US 70 East/Glenwood Ave. After 1 mile, turn right into the park.

BACKUP BASE CAMP

Holly Point Campground (NC State Parks) *14500 New Light Road, Wake Forest; 919-676-1027; ncparks.gov/falls-lake-state-recreation-area/camping. $17–$24/night on weekends, open March 15–October 31, 153 sites, reservations accepted, picnic table, fire ring, tent pad, lantern hook, flush toilets, hot showers, central water, some sites with water and electrical hookups, dump station*

Craving a weekend on the water? Holly Point Campground is located on Falls Lake and many sites have waterfront views/lake access. Your best bet for a waterfront site is Loop 5, but Loop 2 is closest to the designated swimming beach. The campground is only a few minutes away from the New Light and Beaverdam bike trails.

INDOOR LODGING

Hotel Indigo *151 Tatum Dr., Durham; 919-474-3000; ihg.com/hotelindigo/hotels /us/en/durham/rduin/hoteldetail. $90–$150/night, queen and king beds, free Wi-Fi, indoor pool, dogs allowed with $75 fee*

We like our tent better than most chain hotels, but we are fans of Hotel Indigo. It has a fun, quirky decor and comfortable beds, and unlike many "pet-friendly" hotels, the staff actually seems happy to host your four-legged family members.

BIKING

On the trail at Lake Crabtree

MOUNTAIN BIKING

Lake Crabtree County Park *10 miles of trails, short loops, easy–moderate, pump track, jumps, skills features*

The Crabtree trails consist of one larger loop (the Highland Trail) with plenty of short connector trails that allow you to choose your own adventure. Start at the main trailhead, across the road from the boat launch parking area. The trails are mostly fast and flowy fun, while others have some skills features that just might throw you for a loop the first time. Because the connector trails allow for plenty of short loops, it's easy to ride and repeat any sections you really love. No worries about getting lost, as the trails are well marked, and there are signs at the trailheads and most junctions. And while the Crabtree trails are extremely popular, the upside of busy trails is that it's easy to find a local rider to point you in the right direction. You're never far from the parking lot, so it's easy to decide to cruise back whenever you're done. The trails are labeled by difficulty, but a beginner rider with minimal experience could handle everything, even the advanced trails.

■ A jump on the Lake Crabtree trails

Signs forewarn you of upcoming obstacles and there's always a bypass option. The elevation change is minimal and the trails are not physically demanding, so it's easy to ride for hours!

Directions From Umstead, turn left onto Glenwood Ave. (US 70) for 0.9 mile, then take the Westgate Road ramp to I-540. In 0.4 mile, keep left to stay on I-540. Continue on I-540 for 2.4 miles, then take Exit 2 for Aviation Parkway. Stay on Aviation Parkway for 3 miles. Lake Crabtree Park is on the left.

■ New Light trail

New Light Trails *8-mile loop, 2 hours, intermediate–advanced, rock gardens, logs, jumps, lake views, open only on Sundays from September 1–May 14 (hunting season), open daily May 15– August 31, no dogs allowed*

Literally and figuratively, these trails rock. First of all, they're the perfect blend of challenging features and fun flow. And then there are the actual rocks: rock gardens, rock piles, rocks and roots, loose rocks, pointy rocks . . . you get the picture. A lot of local riders show up in kneepads. These aren't beginner trails, but intermediate riders can (carefully) have a good time out here. Begin at the trailhead to the right of the gate, riding the loop counterclockwise. Watch for the white wildlife signs marking the trail. Ride over several rock piles and squeeze through some narrow trail sections. There's some climbing, but nothing gut busting. Around mile 3, at the top of the first sustained climb, the trail comes to a T. Turn left, then take a quick right, watching for the reflectors marking the route. After pushing through, yes, another rock garden, you'll fly downhill. Eyes up! Here, and throughout the loop, there are advanced jumps and features that should be scouted before riding. You can always detour around them; while it's not a hard and fast rule, the bypass is usually on the left. After a relatively smooth lakeside ride, you'll power through (or hike-a-bike) some rocky climbs, tight switchbacks, and substantial rock gardens. When you reach a signed trail junction at a logging road, continue straight ahead on Easy Street. Finish your ride at the gate.

> **Directions** From Umstead, turn left onto US 70/Glenwood Ave. Stay right to continue on I-540 East for 5 miles. Take Exit 9 for NC 50, then turn left onto NC 50 North/Creedmore Road for 5 miles. Exit right onto NC 98 East for 0.5 mile. Turn left onto Ghoston Road for 1 mile, then turn left onto New Light Road. At 2.1 miles, turn left onto Old Weaver Trail (turn is just past a house). Park anywhere off the gravel road.

ADVENTURE WEEKEND HONORABLE MENTIONS

Family Riding Doubletrack at Umstead. Almost 13 miles of gravel road riding, with decent climbing and descending; easily accessible from the multiuse trailhead.

Classic Singletrack Beaverdam Trails at Falls Lake State Recreation Area. Nearly 14 miles of singletrack, mostly made up of short loops. Beginner and intermediate options; experienced riders can play around on the 1-mile Drop Zone. $6/car entry fee, 14600 Creedmore Road, Wake Forest.

> **BIKING NOTE**
>
> You might have heard that there's singletrack riding at Umstead. What people are referring to are the unauthorized trails that are actually on Raleigh-Durham Airport Authority property, beyond the NO TRESPASSING signs near the park's Reedy Creek entrance.

■ Beaverdam Trails

ROAD BIKING

Neuse River Greenway *27.5 miles one-way, easy, Neuse River views, interpretive signs, parks, suspension bridges, boardwalks, wetlands*

■ Signage on the Neuse River Greenway

The Neuse River Greenway Trail is part of the Capital City Greenway, the Mountains-to-Sea Trail, and the East Coast Greenway, making it a quadruple trail whammy! The trail runs north to south from Falls Lake Dam (12088 Falls of Neuse Road) to the Wake County–Johnston County Line (6090 Mial Plantation Road). If you have two cars, it's worth shuttling.

Option two starts at Milburnie Dam, at mile 14.2 on the greenway. Here, you can pedal to either the northern or southern terminus for a 28-plus-mile out-and-back spin. The bonus to this option is that you'll start at the put-in for our recommended Neuse River paddle. Heading north, you'll cross several bridges over the Neuse, have two opportunities for bathroom breaks at local parks, and get a chance to stop at The Bike Guy, a bike shop at Falls Lake Dam. Southbounders will also cross several bridges, ride through scenic pasture, and have the option to ride an extra 4 miles to Clayton, where the trail becomes the Clayton River Walk. (Want to really tack on mileage? Hit up the 18-mile Walnut Creek Trail, just south of Poole Road.) There are a few moderate hills in either direction. Keep in mind that while you'll always find road cyclists doing serious training on the trail, the official speed limit is 10 miles per hour. Look up, communicate kindly, and be respectful of other greenway users.

Directions From Umstead, turn left onto US 70/Glenwood Ave. and go 3 miles to I-540 East. Take I-540 for 8.9 miles to Exit 14, Falls of Neuse Road. Turn left and travel 3.3 miles on Falls of Neuse Road, then turn left onto Old Falls of Neuse Road for 0.5 mile. Just past The Bike Guy, turn left and park at the Falls Lake Dam parking area. To get to the southern terminus, get back on I-540 East for 11.5 miles to Exit 26B, US 264/64 East. Take Exit 425 onto Smithfield Road. Go right on Smithfield for 2.5 miles, then turn right onto Major Slade Road. In 0.5 mile, turn right onto Mial Plantation Road. The parking area is on the right in 2.8 miles, before you cross the river.

The Bike Guy *9745 Fonville Road, Wake Forest; 919-977-5164; thebikeguyonthegreenway.com*

Located at the base of Falls Dam on the Neuse River Greenway, this is a great place to stop if your bike gets a boo-boo, you need a rental, or if you just want to warm up by the wood stove.

Bicycle Chain *9000 Glenwood Ave., Raleigh; 919-782-1000; thebicyclechain.com*

Huge, full-service shop with locations all over the Triangle. For another ride option, check out its weekend group rides. Email thegrouppride@gmail.com for more info.

HIKING

Eno River State Park: Buckquarter Creek/Holden Mill Loop *4.5-mile loop, 2 hours, easy, river, mill ruins, diverse ecosystems*

You can't miss the Buckquarter Creek Trail.

The hiking trails around the Eno River are some of the best for close-to-the-city hiking that doesn't feel like it's anywhere near the city. Check out the park's visitor center before you hit the trail. It's small but mighty, with a staff that's passionate and knowledgeable about the area.

Then follow the signs behind the center to the red-blazed Buckquarter Creek Trail. Follow the gentle terrain of this trail as it follows the Eno River. Around mile 1, you'll reach a junction with Holden Mill Trail. Cross Buckquarter Creek on a sturdy footbridge to follow the yellow-blazed Holden Mill Trail.

Holden Mill is a loop, so you can traverse it in either direction. We recommend turning left, heading upstream on the Eno. At mile 1.5, climb over some large riverside boulders. At mile 2, take a spur trail on the left that leads to the remains of an old mill, one of more than 30 that were located on the Eno until the 1940s. At the end of the spur, continue on the Holden Mill Trail, climbing up and away from the river. At the top of the hill, the trail follows rolling hills over a small ridge, and then heads back down into the floodplain, rejoining Buckquarter Creek Trail. At mile 4, you can turn left to return to the visitor center or continue straight for a quick trip to Fews Ford, a good spot for a history lesson and for wading.

If you'd like, follow the road up from Fews Ford to the 19th-century Piper-Cox House for a taste of colonial life. Take the road back to the visitor center from here, turning left at the T-intersection to return to your car.

Directions From Umstead, turn left onto US 70 West/Glenwood Ave. for 11 miles. Stay left at the fork and merge onto US 70 West/I-85 South for 4.6 miles. Stay left at the fork to stay on 1-85 South. Take Exit 173 for Cole Mill Road, then turn right onto Cole Mill Road. The park is 5.2 miles on the right.

■ History and wading at Fews Ford

West Point on the Eno to Sennett's Hole *1.3 miles round-trip, 45 minutes, easy, swimming hole, mill dam, river views*

Located on the site of a once-thriving mill community on the Eno River, West Point on the Eno offers a little of something for everyone: historical buildings, a natural playscape, 5 miles of hiking trails, and easy paddling.

On summer days, Sennett's Hole, a deep swimming hole created by the Eno's confluence with Warren Creek, is the big draw. To hike to Sennett's, fol-

■ Sennett's Hole

low the yellow-blazed South River Trail from the gravel trailhead near the parking area and the old mill dam. This is probably the best-blazed trail we've ever seen. If you do manage to get off-track (as we somehow did), just stop and look around. You'll rock-hop across a few (usually) small creeks. The creeks swell quickly with rain, so if they don't seem small, use good judgment about crossing. In 0.5 mile, you'll reach the red-blazed Sennett's Hole Trail. Turn right and head upriver. Numerous leg-

ends prevail about Michael Synott, who owned a mill that was swept away at this spot. Many of the tales involve some combination of the Devil, a gold stash, and a bottomless river. While we can't speak authoritatively on any of that, we can tell you that you're likely to encounter yellow-bellied turtles, fresh water clams, and large sycamore trees shading the river. When you've had your fill, return the way you came.

You can also reach Sennett's Hole by paddling upriver. Frog Hollow Outdoors rents kayaks and canoes near the dam, and it's an easy and scenic paddle.

Directions Turn left onto Glenwood Ave./US 70. Continue on US 70 West for 11 miles. Keep left at the fork and merge onto I-85 South/US 70 West for 2 miles. Take Exit 176 for US 501 North/Duke St., continuing on 501 North for 3.3 miles. Turn left onto Seven Oaks Road.

William B. Umstead State Park: Sycamore Trail *5.1-mile loop, 2 hours, easy–moderate, creek valley, old-growth forest*

Sycamore Trail bridge

It's pretty amazing that a park located on the edge of the city has 20-plus miles of trails. The Company Mill Trail and the Sycamore Trail are two of our favorites. However, on nice weekends, Company Mill often resembles a hiker highway, while Sycamore gets far less foot traffic.

We start this particular Sycamore loop at the multiuse trailhead. (The official trailhead for the Sycamore Trail is at the Crabtree Creek entrance off of Glenwood Road, behind Shelter 1. From here, it's a 7.2-mile round-trip.) From the multiuse trailhead, turn right onto the Sycamore Trail. At mile 1, you'll reach a signed junction where the trail comes in from the "official" trailhead. If you're a fan of mountain hiking, this is where the fun begins—rocks and root, ups and downs, and yellow poplar, sycamore, and ancient oak trees towering above. You'll come to a (usually) dry creekbed on the left, then, at mile 2, the trail crosses a footbridge and carves through a creek valley. Follow Sycamore Creek upstream, enjoying views of the dark-green water tumbling over river rocks. At mile 2.4, Sycamore Creek bends around some large rocks; this is a perfect pit stop for a snack or swim. At mile 3.1, you'll reach the Sycamore Creek Bridge at the intersection with the Graylynn Trail; watch for cyclists and horses. Continue straight. At mile 4.1, get your last glimpse of Sycamore Creek and start hiking uphill. When you reach the junction you passed earlier, stay left to return to the trailhead and congratulate yourself on hiking the trail less taken.

Directions From the campground, head past the visitor center. Turn left onto Maintenance Road, then right onto Group Camp Road and left onto Sycamore Road.

PADDLING ⊗

For a cheap, easy, and family-friendly paddle, rent a canoe or rowboat from Umstead for use on Big Lake. If you want to check out the local river scene, keep in mind that much of the whitewater paddling around here is heavily dependent on water levels.

WHITEWATER

Neuse River, Milburnie Dam to Poole Road *3.5-mile run, Class I–II, put in at Milburnie Dam, take out at Poole Road.*

The first time we ran this convenient, close-to-the city stretch, we were a little concerned that it would be a paddling superhighway. However, the last Saturday we paddled here we only had to share the river with a group practicing rescues, a rare wood stork, and a lot of turtles. It was quite peaceful, which is appropriate because we later learned that the river was named after the Neusiock Indians (Neusiock means "peace"). While some traffic noise does filter through the surrounding woods, this isn't your typical urban paddle: you'll see a lot more greenway than roadway.

Put in below the dam, and just downriver veer left around a small island. This is a beginner-friendly paddle, but, as always, keep an eye out for boat-swamping strainers. You'll have plenty of time to maneuver around them as long as you scout ahead. Around mile 2.5, Crabtree Creek comes in on the right. Half a mile downriver, watch for a house on the right. This is the site of the magic rapid. When the river is running low, a stretch of boulders creates a manageable Class II rapid. Stay to the left. When the river level is up, the rapid

Milburnie Dam

disappears and all you'll see are some small ripples. At mile 3.5, just before the Poole Road overpass, watch for a Neuse River Greenway sign on the right by the takeout. You couldn't ask for a better place to self-shuttle. You can lock your boat to the stand at the top of the boat launch, then take a 4-mile run on the scenic Neuse River Greenway to the put-in. A bike shuttle would work equally well. If you'd rather be shuttled, contact Frog Hollow Outfitters or Paddle Creek.

Directions to put-in From William B. Umstead State Park, turn left onto Glenwood Ave./US 70, then take the Westgate Road ramp to I-540. Merge onto I-540 East for 18.9 miles, then take Exit 24A for US 64 Business West. Turn right and continue on US 64 business West for 0.8 mile. Turn right onto Old Milburnie Road, then take the first left onto Loch Raven Parkway. Turn right onto an access road past a power station and continue to the parking area on river left.

Directions to takeout From the put-in, head back to US 64 and turn left. Before you get to I-540, turn right onto Hodge Road. Follow Hodge Road for 3.1 miles to the intersection with Poole Road. Turn right onto Poole Road for 1 mile. Cross the Neuse River, then find Poole Road Park immediately on your right.

FLATWATER

Three Rivers Area at the Eno Boat Launch *Out-and-back paddles of variable distances, put-in at Eno Boat Launch, lake, river, and creek paddling*

The western section of Falls Lake is where the Eno, Flat, and Little Rivers converge to form the headwaters of the Neuse River. It offers great one-stop lake, river, and creek paddling, and it's a good spot to seek solitude. Even on picture-perfect days when everyone wants to be on the water, there are tons of quiet coves and creeks. From the boat launch, you can head left (downstream) or right (upstream) on the Eno. Heading downriver, the Flat River flows in on the left within the first mile. You can paddle up the Flat for about 6 miles before the current will not-so-gently suggest that you turn around. You can also paddle 3 miles right (upriver) from the boat ramp to explore the Little River, which enters on the right. Whatever direction you go, take advantage of small sandy banks where you can park your boat for a break, snack, or swim.

> *Directions to put-in* From William B. Umstead State Park, turn left onto Glenwood Ave./US 70 for 11 miles. Take the ramp for I-85 North, and travel 3.7 miles to Exit 182, Red Mill Road. Turn left onto Red Mill Road and drive 3.7 miles to Teknica Parkway. Turn right onto Teknica, then right again at Red Mill Road. The parking area is at the end of Red Mill Road.

ADVENTURE WEEKEND HONORABLE MENTIONS

Sunset Paddle Hickory Hill boat ramp on Falls Lake. 4601 Redwood Road, Durham.

Paddle and Swim Jordan Lake. Bald eagles and sandy swimming beaches; use Ebenezer Church Boat Ramp or Weaver Creek Access. See ncparks.gov for directions—GPS is misleading.

OUTFITTERS

Frog Hollow Outdoors *614 Trent Dr., Durham; 919-416-1200; froghollowoutdoors.com*

Canoe, kayak, and SUP rentals; shuttle services (call for availability); variety of guided trips. The staff know this area well and are willing to share their expertise.

Paddle Creek *9601 Capital Blvd., Wake Forest; 919-866-1954; paddlecreeknc.com*

Self-guided trips down the Neuse, private takeout, kayak, canoe, and SUP rentals, shuttles.

MAPS

Maps for William B. Umstead State Park, West Point on the Eno, Lake Crabtree, and Eno River State Park are available at the parks and on their respective websites. Pick up a map for the Neuse River Trail at kiosks along the trail or at raleighnc.gov.

RAINY DAY 😎

Wells Fargo IMAX Theater *201 East Hargett St., Raleigh; 919-882-IMAX; imaxraleigh.org*

It's never fun to get rained out, but the adventure can continue in 3-D on the giant screen. You're sure to find a nature-themed showing, and the theater is located in the Marbles Kids Museum. See website for pricing and showtimes.

FOOD AND DRINK 🍺

Crank Arm Brewing *319 W. Davie St., Raleigh; 919-324-3529; crankarmbrewing.com*

You dream of bikes and beer, they dream of bikes and beer. Their impressive selection of seasonal beers is balanced by their reserve of classic brews. The Unicycle is a true uniter of all beer tastes. Tons of indoor and outdoor seating.

Lonerider Brewing Company *8816 Gulf Court, Ste. 100, Raleigh; 919-442-8004; loneriderbeer.com*

Because: it's less than 2 miles from Umstead. Need another reason? You'll get hooked on the smooth Sweet Josie Brown Ale, which is just fine because it comes in adventure-friendly cans.

Relish Café and Bar *5625 Creedmoor Road, Raleigh; 919-787-1855; relishraleigh.com*

Among its extensive menu offerings: a salsa flight, mac and cheese skillets, and homemade donuts, made to order. Busy on Sundays for brunch/lunch, but worth the wait.

GEAR AND RESUPPLY 🛒

REI *4291 The Circle at North Hills St., Raleigh; 919-571-5031; rei.com/stores/raleigh*

You know what REI is. Everything you need and don't need for the outdoors. Wallets, beware.

Crank Arm Brewing

Bradley Falls

SALUDA

Want to adventure where the pros play? Saluda's world-class adventures are no secret to top-notch athletes, but there's plenty of outdoor fun for amateurs too. So much, in fact, that we planned on visiting Saluda for a day . . . and ended up staying for a weekend. Camp along the Green River, where professional kayakers, tube-toting families, and everyone in between can enjoy a day on the water. Hike and mountain bike in near solitude in the 10,000-acre Green River Gamelands. Nearby Rumbling Bald offers world-class bouldering, and Saluda's hilly, rural roads are ripe for road biking. Keep that adrenaline pumping and rappel down Big Bradley Falls or zipline through the Green River Gorge's treetops. In between adventures, enjoy the laid-back, friendly vibe of Saluda, located at the top of the steepest mainland railroad grade east of the Rocky Mountains.

Areas included: Green River, Green River Gamelands, Rumbling Bald

Adventures: Camping, mountain and road biking, hiking, bouldering, rappelling, whitewater paddling, ziplining

SALUDA

1. Big Rock River Access
2. Bishop Branch Trailhead
3. Blue Firefly Inn
4. Fishtop River Access
5. Gorge Zipline Canopy Adventure
6. Green River Adventures
7. Green River Brew Depot
8. Green River Cove XC Course Trailhead
9. Orchard Lake Campground
10. Pace Mountain–Pearson's Glen Loop Start
11. Pulliam Creek Trailhead
12. Purple Onion
13. Rumbling Bald Access
14. Team ECCO Ocean Center and Aquarium
15. Thompson's Store
16. Wilderness Cove Tubing and Campground
17. Wildflour Bakery

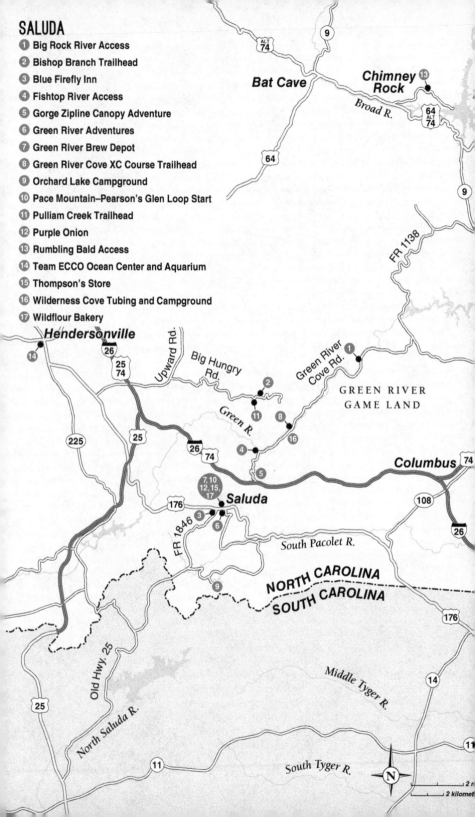

LODGING ⛺

TOP PICK

WILDERNESS COVE CAMPGROUND (PRIVATE) *3773 Green River Cove Road, Saluda; 828-749-9100; wildernesscovecampground.com. $20+/night, open mid-March–October 31, 16 sites, reservations accepted, picnic table, fire ring, tent pad, flush toilets, hot showers, some sites share central water, some sites with water and electric for an additional fee, tubing trips*

River rats, this is your home away from home on the Green River. Located riverside, Wilderness Cove is only 1.3 miles from the Fishtop put-in. But paddlers don't get to have all the fun at this little campground. Hike to Big Bradley Falls or explore the Green Cove Trail, by boot or bike, straight from your site. The sites are small, but think of them as the campsite version of a tiny house. You'll have just enough space for

everything you need to camp comfortably: a level, well-graveled tent pad (*just big enough for a six-man tent*), picnic table, fire ring, and lots of tree canopy. We recommend grabbing a creekside site, if you can. If you're going for privacy and space, choose site 6 or 7, or snag one of the bigger (but less shaded) sites with water and electric.

Directions From I-26, take Exit 59 to Saluda. If coming from the east (South Carolina), turn right. If coming from the west (Asheville), turn left. Take the first left onto Green River Cove Road, which descends steeply around 17 tight switchbacks. The campground is 3.4 miles on the right.

■ Creekside site at Wilderness Cove Campground

BACKUP BASE CAMP

Orchard Lake Campground (private) *460 Orchard Lake Road, Saluda; 828-749-3901; orchardlakecampground.com. $35+/night, open April–October, 130 sites, reservations accepted, picnic table, fire ring, flush toilets, showers, water and electric at sites, Wi-Fi, swimming lake, boats, small zipline, playground and outdoor games*

If Wilderness Cove is full or you have epically energetic kids, Orchard Lake is your place. The campground is about a 30-minute drive to the Green River Gamelands, but there's plenty of kid-friendly adventuring here to keep the family busy.

INDOOR LODGING

Blue Firefly Inn *91 Greenville St., Saluda; 828-808-4248; bluefireflyinn.com. $130–$180/night, Wi-Fi, queen and twin beds, private baths, bike work station, outdoor shower and bike wash, guided bike rides, local art, breakfast included*

This newly restored historic house-turned-inn is the perfect place for you and your bike to reconnect. (Of course, your family and friends are welcome too.) The owner knows what adventurers need—nourishing food, local adventure beta, and one room with four extra-large twin beds so that you and your adventure buddies never have to be apart.

BIKING ⏩

MOUNTAIN BIKING

Mountain biking is relatively new to the Green River Gamelands, but these well-built trails are getting more attention from the rest of the mountain biking world since the introduction of the Green River Games multisport competition in 2013.

Green River Games XC Course *8-mile loop, 1.5–2.5 hours, moderate–difficult, river views, race course*

Start on the Green River Cove Trail at Bradley Cemetery, just downstream from Wilderness Cove Campground. The trail begins on a steep set of stairs. We've carefully ridden down these stairs, but there's no shame in a little hike-a-bike on the way up!

Green River Cove Trail

■ Green River Narrows

Just past the stairs, you'll crest a punchy climb at the junction with the Bluff Trail on the right. Continue on the Green River Cove Trail, which alternates between hugging the riverbank and climbing steeply over ridges high above the water. Climb another set of steep stairs, either on or off your bike. At this point, the trail follows the river more faithfully to its junction with the Pulliam Creek Trail at mile 2.75. Turn right onto the Pulliam Creek Trail. Continue past the junction with the Bear Branch Trail on the right and climb gradually along the side of a ridge.

In the next mile, look for several steep foot trails on the left that lead downhill to the Green River Narrows. If you choose to hike one of these side trails, be careful. (See the Pulliam Creek Trail hike description on pages 142–143 for details.) Continue another 2 miles on the Green River Cove Trail to the junction with the Rock Hop Trail on the right. Turn right on Rock Hop and ride 0.5 mile. Turn right onto Bishop Branch Trail, climbing to a junction with the Bear Branch Trail. Turn left at Bear Branch, and within 0.25 mile, turn right onto Long Ridge Trail. Continue 0.3 mile, and then turn left onto Stair Step Falls. Follow the top of a ridge downhill and past a scramble-access to the falls near the end of the trail. At the junction with the Turkey Gut Trail, turn right and travel 0.25 mile before taking a right onto the Bluff Trail. Bluff is STEEP and you may find yourself hike-a-biking downhill on this gnarly trail. After 1 mile, turn left onto the Green River Cove Trail and head back down the stairs to complete this epic loop.

Directions From Wilderness Cove Campground, turn right onto Green River Cove Road. Just past the bridge over the river, look for the trailhead on the left.

Bear Branch Downhill *6-mile loop, 1.5 hours, moderate–difficult, long descent, river views*

Start at the Bishop Branch Trailhead along Big Hungry Road and ride south for 1.25 miles. Continue past the Rock Hop Trail on the right at mile 0.6, and then turn right onto the Bear Branch Trail. For the next 1.5 miles, climb Bear Branch Trail onto a ridge and then head down, down, down to its terminus at the Pulliam Creek Trail. This descent is one of the best in the Green River Gamelands, so enjoy! At the end of Bear Branch, catch your breath and turn right onto the Pulliam Creek Trail (see description of the Pulliam Creek Trail in the Green River XC Course). Ride uphill for 2.75 miles, and then turn right onto the Rock Hop Trail. At the Bishop Branch Trail, turn left and head back to your vehicle.

> **Directions** From Saluda, take I-26 west. Take the second exit onto Upward Road. Turn right onto Upward Road and continue 1.8 miles. Turn right onto Big Hungry Road. Almost immediately, turn left to stay on Big Hungry Road. After the bridge, the Bishop Branch Trailhead is 2.4 miles down the road on the right.

ROAD BIKING

Put on your climbing pants—or bibs—and get ready for some major elevation change. The riding around here is hilly, to say the least, but the scenery is phenomenal and you'll have long stretches of road to yourself.

■ Downtown Saluda

Pace Mountain/Pearson's Glen Loop *18.5 miles, 1.5 hours, moderate, Pearson's Glen, 2,100-plus feet of climbing*

This ride starts on Saluda's Main St. It's hilly, but none of the climbs are truly brutal and you can begin or end your ride with a stop at Wildflour Bakery.

- Start by going west on Main St., and then turn right onto Church St., just past the Purple Onion.
- Mile 0.4: Left onto East Columbus St., then immediate right onto Henderson St.
- Mile 0.6: Veer right onto Esseola St., riding past Bradley Nature Reserve. Enjoy the downhill!
- Mile 1.3: Left onto Howard Gap Road.
- Mile 3.4: Continue straight on Macedonia Road.

- Mile 5.8: Left onto Pace Mountain Road.
- Mile 8.0: Left onto Mountain Page Road.
- Mile 8.5: Sharp right onto L.M. Morgan Road, then immediate right onto Old Mountain Page Road.
- Mile 9.8: Left onto Mountain Page Road.
- Mile 10.1: Slight left onto Mine Mountain Road.
- Mile 11.6: Left onto West Fork Creek Road.
- Mile 13.5: Left onto Fork Creek Road.
- Mile 15.2: Left onto Pearson Falls Road. Start a scenic ride past Pearson's Glen. There's a sustained but manageable climb back to town from here.
- Mile 18.4: Left onto East Main St. Is there a recovery cinnamon bun calling your name?

HIKING ⬤

Bradley Falls Trail *4.4-mile out-and-back, 2 hours, moderate, falls, creekside hiking, wildflowers.*

■ On the trail to Bradley Falls

While many hikers take the shorter route to Bradley Falls from the top, we prefer approaching the falls from below. It's a longer hike and the trail is not signed or maintained, but you'll be rewarded with more solitude and, in our opinion, better views.

Head past the gate on the gravel road, taking in views of the Green River on your left. The road veers away from the river and passes several fields on the left. Look up to take in views of Cove Mountain to the south and Raccoon Mountain to the north. At mile 1, pass an old barn on your left. Where the dirt road turns left around the barn, head straight ahead toward the treeline, passing another small barn on the right. Here, the trail turns right and parallels the creek, and then flanks another field before finally reaching the forest. While not officially signed, the trail is marked with brightly colored marking tape tied to trees. With the creek on your left, follow the now-obvious trail to an easy creek crossing, just past mile 1.5. The trail gets a little elusive here. Past the creek, keep to the left and look for marking tape. Even if you do get off-track,

■ Bradley Falls

the forest is rather open here, so getting back on track isn't difficult.

The gentle part of the hike is now behind you, as you start climbing up and away from the creek. Watch your step, as there are places where the trail is barely hanging on to the steep terrain. Wildflowers surround the trail in the spring and summer months; you can't miss the trillium and fire pinks. At mile 2.25, continue your scramble up to the base of Big Bradley Falls. We strongly urge you to enjoy the view from the bottom, as many reckless adventurers have died while attempting to scale the falls. If you want some safe vertical time on the falls, check out the rappelling trip offered by Green River Adventures.

Directions Follow directions to Wilderness Cove Campground. Go left at the campground parking lot. The road will dead-end at the parking area for the trailhead.

Pulliam Creek Trail to the Narrows *3.2-mile out-and-back, 2–3 hours, moderate-strenuous, swimming hole, creekside hiking, Green River Narrows's Monster Mile*

This hike is a 30-minute drive from the Green River Gorge, but you get unrivaled views of the Narrows, and except for the scramble down to the river, it's an easy hike with minimal elevation change.

From the trailhead on Big Hungry Road, cross a small footbridge to access the blue-blazed Pulliam Creek Trail. (Keep an eye out for some creative blazes.) At 0.5 mile, the Rock Hop Trail enters on the left. Continue straight, passing a farm track that heads uphill on the right. Enjoy another 0.5 mile of gentle descending to a creek crossing. Rock-hop across the water and watch for a swimming hole just past the crossing.

At 1.4 miles, look for a trail that appears to fall off the side of the mountain on your right. The good news: This is the fastest way down to the Narrows. The bad news: Fast doesn't mean easy! This slippery, rocky, and loose 0.2-mile "trail" drops straight down to the river, with ropes placed to help keep you upright. We only recommend this scramble for those in good physical condition. Keep in mind that, for better or worse, gravity will assist you with your descent but will work against you when it's time to climb back up. At the bottom, the trail rejoins the mouth of Pulliam Creek, where a quick rock hop leads you to the massive boulders and thundering water of the Green River Narrows.

The churning whitewater on display in front of you is the playground for the best kayakers from all over the world. These boaters come for the high-risk challenge of running this 2.8-mile section of the river with continuous Class IV, V, and V+ rapids. Walk carefully toward the river for views of the Monster Mile. Here, the river, already quite narrow at this point, barrels over a waterfall and onto boulders at a rate of 350 feet per mile. You'll have a great view of Sunshine Falls from here, but you can also carefully maneuver upstream and check out other rapids with appropriately intimidating names like Nutcracker, Green Scream Machine, and Gorilla.

Every year, on the first Saturday of November, the world's best paddlers convene to compete in the Green River Race, the epitome of extreme kayak racing. Even if other hikers join you to enjoy the show, the roar of the powerful water, surrounded by 1,000-foot canyon walls, will make you feel quite alone—and small—in this very wild place. When you're ready, scramble back up the access trail and turn left on the Pulliam Creek Trail to return to the trailhead.

> **Directions** From Saluda, take I-26 west. Take the second exit onto Upward Road. Turn right onto Upward Road and continue 1.8 miles. Turn right onto Big Hungry Road. Almost immediately, turn left to stay on Big Hungry Road. The trailhead is on the right, about 2 miles after crossing the bridge over Big Hungry Creek. Watch for a very small roadside parking area and a wooden bridge that leads to the trail. If you reach the trailhead for Bishop Branch or Long Ridge, you've gone too far.

PADDLING ⊗

The Green River is a beloved whitewater oasis that offers something for all paddlers. World-class kayakers can take the run of their lives on the Class IV–V+ rapids of the Green River Narrows. Experienced paddlers with solid skills can challenge themselves on the Upper Green's Class III+ drops and rapids. (If this is your first run on the Upper Green, we recommend bringing an experienced friend or contacting Green River Adventures for beta or guide service.) Our top pick for a Green River paddle is the fun-for-all Lower Green.

> **NOTE**
>
> North Carolina state law forbids alcohol within 100 feet of the river. The law is strictly enforced, so no ca-brewing. This ordinance has immensely improved river quality and the paddling experience on the Green in recent years.

■ Canoeing on the Lower Green

Lower Green River *6-mile run, Class I–II, put in at Fishtop Access, take out at Big Rock Access, ample parking at put-in and takeout*

The Green is a dam-fed river, and Duke Energy typically releases water into the river from Lake Summit at 7 a.m. Spend the morning adventuring on dry land (or sleeping), as the water takes 4 hours to reach the Fishtop Access. The river is generally runnable year-round and can get a bit rowdy after a strong rain. This stretch has numerous Class I–II rapids, with just the right amount of time between wave trains to grab a snack, gawk at the scenery, scout the next wave train, or recover your equipment after an unplanned swim. Around the halfway mark, there's a small sandbar on the right. The water is deep and fast here; it's a good spot to take a dip and eat lunch. You won't completely escape civilization, as the river runs alongside Green Cove Road and numerous houses line the riverbanks, but there's enough natural beauty to make up for it. The river is named for the gorgeous green hue of its waters (although after heavy rains, Brown River might be a more appropriate moniker). Watch for the yellow tubing sign about 1.5 miles past the second bridge, where you'll find the Big Rock takeout on river right. The local outfitters don't offer regular shuttle services, but it's easy to self-shuttle by bike if you don't have two cars.

Directions to put-in From I-26, take Exit 59 (Saluda). If coming from the east (South Carolina), turn right. If coming from the west (Asheville), turn left. Take the first left onto Green River Cove Road, which descends steeply around tight switchbacks. Put-in is about 2.5 miles on the left.

Directions to takeout From Fishtop, turn left onto Green River Cove Road. Big Rock takeout is 6 miles on your left.

Green River Adventures *111 East Main St., Saluda; 800-335-1530;*
greenriveradventures.com

Kayak and SUP rentals, guided trips, kayak instruction.

CLIMBING 🖉

Rumbling Bald Bouldering *Best in fall, winter, and spring; southern exposure; V0–V8*

Chimney Rock State Park, which includes the Rumbling Bald area, was once a private tourist attraction, but it was purchased by the state in 2007 and is run as a pay-to-play park in the model of Grandfather Mountain to the northeast. Rumbling Bald, however, offers a less groomed mountain experience and, as a result, access to it is free. From the towns of Lake Lure and Chimney Rock, look north to see the sheer face of Rumbling Bald, which offers outstanding single-pitch sport climbing, a rarity in North Carolina. These cliffs were created by the calving of huge chunks of gneiss, in the process producing boulders that we think are truly adventure weekend–worthy. Recent land acquisitions in the formerly contested area opened it to climbers. Obeying all rules and regulations is both respectful and self-serving, as there are still ongoing access negotiations. There is no camping anywhere in the Rumbling Bald area and the gate closes at sunset, so plan accordingly. We've been lucky enough to enjoy a half day of bouldering in August, but generally speaking, heat, poison ivy, and bugs make this spot a cooler-weather destination. It's about a 40-minute drive from the Green River Gorge, but it is well worth the trip.

There are three distinct bouldering areas: West Side Boulders, Central Boulders, and East Side Boulders, helpfully named according to their orientation. Only have time for one? Head to West Side, which has the highest concentration of easily accessible boulders. Starting from the back of the parking area, follow the new access loop trail and turn left where the trail splits. Continue to a marked trail on your left and follow this trail up to the bouldering area. It's easy to scout here and explore the rich variety of cracks, slabs, and overhang problems that lay scattered along the base of the cliffs. The gneiss that makes up these rocks was cooked hot and hard, making it almost like granite in terms of its stiffness and grip, so chalk up and trust the rubber in your shoes. If you plan to spend an entire weekend (or longer) playing around on rock and crash pads, we recommend splurging on a copy of *Rumbling Bald Bouldering, 2nd Edition,* by Chris Dorrity.

■ Rumbling Bald

Directions From Wilderness Cove Campground, turn right onto Green River Cove Road and travel 7 miles. Turn right on Silver Creek Road. In 2 miles, turn left onto Garret Road. In 1.3 miles, reach a T-junction with NC 9. Turn left and travel north 6.6 miles, then turn left onto US 74/64 West, through the town of Lake Lure. In 4 miles, turn right onto Boys Camp Road. If you get to the entrance to Chimney Rock Park, you've gone too far. Follow Boys Camp Road for 1.4 miles and look for the Rumbling Bald Access Road on the left. Take the access road to the parking area and hit the rocks.

VERTICAL ADVENTURES

Green River Adventures *111 E. Main St., Saluda; 800-335-1530; greenriveradventures.com*

This is your one-stop shop for guided adventures, from mild to wild. We recommend booking one of the Bradley Falls rappelling trips. If you're not sure how you feel about lowering yourself down the side of a cliff into a waterfall, try the shorter rappel down the 70-foot Little Bradley Falls (minimum age: 12). Ready to go all out? Those age 15 and above can rappel the 200-foot Big Bradley Waterfall.

The Gorge Zipline Canopy Adventure
166 Honey Bee Dr., Saluda; 855-749-2500; thegorgezipline.com

With Gorge Zipline Canopy Adventure, sister company to Green River Adventures, you can soar from tree to tree through 1.25 miles of spectacular gorge scenery, conquer three free rappels, and cross a 95-foot suspension bridge. Participants must be at least 10 years old or weigh 70 pounds.

MAPS

Green River Gamelands Trails and Area The Mountain Bike Project has trail descriptions and a basic overview map at mtbproject.com/directory/8013357. Blue Ridge Heritage has a very decent printable PDF trail map at blueridgeheritage .com/sites/default/files/images/greenriver_gamelands_map.pdf.

The North Carolina Wildlife Resources Commission manages this area and provides an area overview booklet that contains a small map of trails, put-ins, access points, and so on at tinyurl.com/greenrvrgl.

RAINY DAY

Team ECCO Ocean Center and Aquarium *511 N. Main St., Hendersonville; 828-692-8386; teamecco.org*

This aquatic educational center is small but mighty, with friendly and knowledgeable staff. One might claim that touch tanks are for tots, but who doesn't like getting up close with turtles, starfish, and horseshoe crabs? There's shark feeding twice a day too. Closed Sundays, $4 per person.

FOOD AND DRINK 🍴

The Purple Onion *16 Main St., Saluda; 828-749-1179; purpleonionsaluda.com*

Head outside to dine on the covered patio . . . that is, if you can make it past the siren call of the homemade desserts near the front door. It offers Mediterranean-inspired cuisine made with local meats and vegetables, and seafood selections as well. Too adventured-out for decisions? Go ahead and order the flatbread of the day, which is always loaded with in-season veggies. Live music most weekends.

Green River Brew Depot *26 Church St., Saluda; 828-808-2600*

Choose from more than a dozen local beers on tap and tons of bottled beers and wine too. Grab a seat on the back porch and enjoy the welcoming vibe. Super friendly to adventure dogs and their people, including kiddos.

Wildflour Bakery *173 E. Main St., Saluda; 828-749-3356; wildflourbakerync.com*

Rolling into town on Friday night? Lucky you—that's pizza night at the bakery. Don't worry if you miss it, though, because the bakery is also the perfect post–road ride Saturday morning stop . . . but only if you love hot-from-the-oven cinnamon rolls. Grab breakfast (available all day) or lunch, or just stop in for a loaf of fresh bread. Wildflour grinds their own flour and bakes daily, so their breads are nutrition-packed loaves of adventure fuel.

GEAR AND RESUPPLY 🛒

On your way into town, stop at the Marathon Gas Station at Exit 59 off I-26, where you can grab convenience store basics and—because this is North Carolina—fill up a growler from their taps. You'll pass a Dollar General on your way to town too. You can get basic groceries in downtown Saluda, but if you forgot your tent, boots, or bike gear, head to downtown Hendersonville, 20 minutes away from Saluda, where you'll find a Mast General Store and Sycamore Cycles.

Thompson's Store *24 Main St., Saluda; 828-749-2322; thompsons-store.com*

It's the oldest grocery store in America! Luckily for us, though the store recently celebrated its 125th anniversary, its selections have kept up with the times. Grab s'more supplies for the kids; while you're there, you might as well check out their extensive craft beer selection.

Pilot Mountain

SAURATOWN MOUNTAINS

The Piedmont's Sauratown Mountains are often referred to as the mountains away from the mountains. However, we think that any place with 2,000-plus-foot peaks, towering rock cliffs, miles of rugged hiking trails, waterfalls, and Class I–II paddling is a mountain in its own right! With two amazing state parks within half an hour of one another, the Sauratowns' outdoor adventures are easily accessible. Camp, climb, paddle, and bike in the 7,869-acre expanse of Hanging Rock State Park. Pilot Mountain State Park offers plenty of hiking and paddling, and climbers often bounce between the two parks to get in as much rock time as possible. Throw in some zipline action and riverside brews, and you've got yourself a true adventure weekend, North Carolina Piedmont-style.

Areas included: Dan River, Danbury, Hanging Rock State Park, Mount Airy, Pilot Mountain State Park, Yadkin River

Adventures: Camping, mountain and road biking, hiking, climbing, flat and whitewater paddling, living history, ziplining

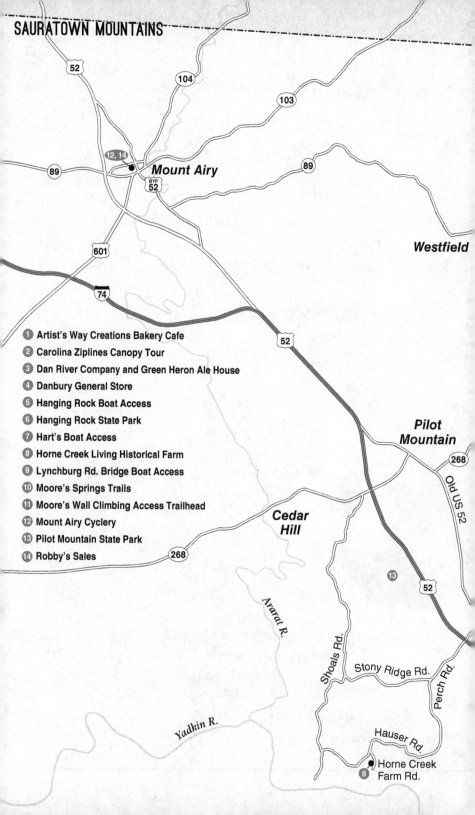

52

104

103

89

89

Mount Airy

12, 14

BYP
52

Westfield

601

74

52

**Pilot
Mountain**

268

Old US 52

1 Artist's Way Creations Bakery Cafe
2 Carolina Ziplines Canopy Tour
3 Dan River Company and Green Heron Ale House
4 Danbury General Store
5 Hanging Rock Boat Access
6 Hanging Rock State Park
7 Hart's Boat Access
8 Horne Creek Living Historical Farm
9 Lynchburg Rd. Bridge Boat Access
10 Moore's Springs Trails
11 Moore's Wall Climbing Access Trailhead
12 Mount Airy Cyclery
13 Pilot Mountain State Park
14 Robby's Sales

**Cedar
Hill**

268

13

52

Ararat R.

Shoals Rd.

Stony Ridge Rd.

Perch Rd.

Yadkin R.

Hauser Rd.

8 Horne Creek
Farm Rd.

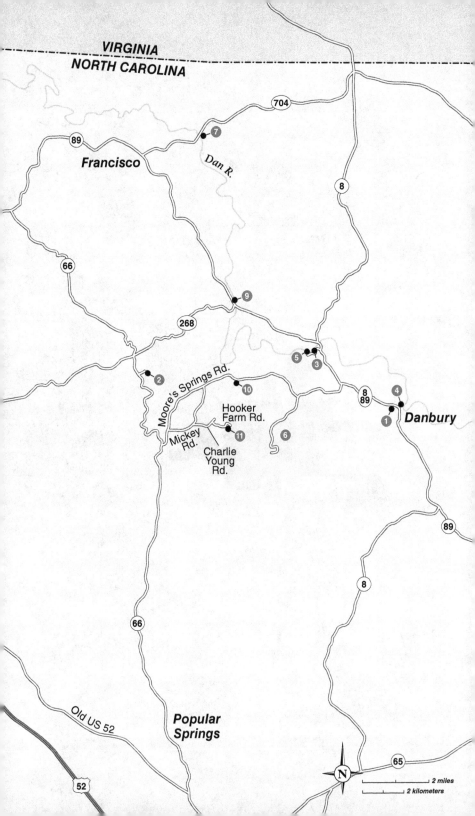

TOP PICK

HANGING ROCK STATE PARK (NC STATE PARKS) *1790 Hanging Rock Park Road, Danbury; 336-593-8480; ncparks.gov/hanging-rock-state-park. $17/night, open year-round, 73 sites, reservations accepted, picnic table, fire ring, tent pad, flush toilets, central water and hot showers (bathhouses closed December 1–March 15; pit toilet available)*

Camping at Hanging Rock State Park feels a little wild, even though you have all your basic camping amenities right on hand. The campground sits high on a ridge and sites are tucked into a forest of mature oak, hickory, maple, and pine trees.

The lower loop (sites 43–73) is open year-round. Sites on the right-hand side of this loop have a wooded "backyard" and offer phenomenal views of the Sauratown Mountains. The most luxurious sites, however, are in the upper loop, which is open mid-March–mid-November. In case you need an excuse to bring more gear, these sites are huge, and some are nestled so far back in the woods that they're hidden from the road. In either loop, though, you can hike straight from your site. You

■ Sun rising over the Sauratown Mountains

will have to make a short drive to access the park's climbing, mountain biking, and whitewater opportunities—Hanging Rock has a lot of land—but it's worth it. Campers must arrive before closing; check website or call for hours.

Directions From Winston-Salem, take NC 8 North to Danbury. Turn left at Pioneer Hospital on Hanging Rock Park Road and continue 1.5 miles.

BACKUP BASE CAMP

Pilot Mountain State Park (NC State Parks) *1792 Pilot Knob Park Road, 336-325-2355, ncparks.gov/pilot-mountain-state-park. $17/night, open March 15–November 30, 49 sites, reservations accepted, picnic table, fire ring, flush toilets, hot showers, shared water*

■ Pilot Mountain

Some might say that the sites here are on the small side, but we prefer to think of them as charmingly cozy. We like that they're built to coexist with the rocky, hilly terrain, rather than totally conquering it. Plus, you can hit the trails straight from your site. Heads up, climbers—you're less than 2 miles from the cliffs.

INDOOR LODGING

Hanging Rock State Park Cabins *1790 Hanging Rock Park Road; 336-593-8480; ncparks.gov/sites/default/files/ncparks/37/hanging-rock-cabin.pdf. $85/night, two bedrooms with two single beds, pullout sofa bed, kitchen with pots, pans, and dinnerware for six, grill, heat and air-conditioning, bathroom, no pets*

These basic cabins, located near the park's campground, are bright, clean, comfortable, and close to trails. What we love: the screened-in porches with rocking chairs.

BIKING ⊘

MOUNTAIN BIKING

The Hanging Rock bike trails—often referred to as the Moore's Springs Trails—aren't located on the main park property, and because they lack the typical state park signage they are a bit tricky to find. Worth it? Definitely.

Moore's Springs Trails *8.4 miles, 1–1.5 hours, intermediate, berms, rock gardens, log bridges, views of Moore's Wall*

A former nature preserve, the Moore's Springs trail system was acquired by the North Carolina state park system in 2014. Thanks to collaborative efforts between the parks department, local riders, and volunteers, the trail system is thriving, and additional beginner and advanced trails are in the works. The current trails are legitimate intermediate trails (read: definitely not for first-time riders), with plenty of opportunities to power through rock gardens, roll over boulders, and test riders' balance on logs and pipes strategically placed over streams. Well-built berms allow advanced riders to fly around curves and the less-than-advanced to maneuver around tricky switchbacks without having to stop. The terrain offers lots of variation, with moderate climbs followed by screaming downhills, and tight and twisty sections that open up into wide, smooth-as-butter trails. The trails are multidirectional and every local rider seems to have a firm opinion on which route is better; we vote clockwise. The rock gardens are easier this way, and we get a kick out of riding up Major Tom and then zooming downhill to Ground Control.

Trailhead at Moore's Springs

To get started, park in the field next to the abandoned barn. Don't be fooled by the primitive trailhead—the trails, which start to the right of the barn, are well marked and immaculately maintained. Head left on the blue-blazed Original Loop. Within the first 0.5 mile, turn left onto the orange-blazed Major Tom Trail. This is the most substantial climb of the ride, but conjure your inner David Bowie power and know you'll be rewarded at the top with views of Moore's Wall. Continue on Major Tom 1.3 miles, then turn left onto the white-blazed Land of the Lost Trail. Follow Land of the Lost for 2 miles. At the junction of Land of the Lost and Original Loop, turn left for some fast, swoopy fun back to the trailhead. Just on the other side of Moore's Springs Road you'll find the 2.1-mile North Side Trail, best ridden counterclockwise. This is a newer and rougher trail, but still worth a ride.

> **Directions** From Hanging Rock State Park, turn left onto Moore's Springs Road. After 2.2 miles, look for a small, weathered brown barn (the Farmhouse) on the left. Address is 2617 Moore's Springs Road, Westfield.

ROAD BIKING

Hanging Rock Almost-Triathlon Route *16 miles, 1.5 hours, moderate–difficult, scenic roads, 2,000 feet of climbing*

There was a triathlon scheduled to be at Hanging Rock State Park in 2016. It was cancelled, however, due to lack of participants. Maybe it had something to do with the 2,000 feet of climbing in the bike leg? If the thought makes your quads quiver in anticipation, give this difficult but scenic ride a go.

- Start at the top of Hanging Rock Campground Road.
- Mile 0.7: Turn left onto Hanging Rock Park Road. Enjoy the descent . . . you'll pay the piper at the end of the ride!
- Mile 2.5: Turn left onto Moore's Springs Road.
- Mile 5.1: Turn right onto Dan George Road.
- Mile 7.2: Turn right onto NC 268 East.
- Mile 8.0: Cross over the Dan River, then turn right onto NC 89 East. Just before mile 10, you'll cruise downhill on a tight and twisty section of road that we've heard referred to as the Gecko Tail. Ride carefully.
- Mile 12.2: Turn right onto Hanging Rock State Park Road. There are two substantial climbs in the final 3 miles. Climb from miles 12–13, and then enjoy a 0.75-mile break before getting your adventure on for the last 900 feet of climbing.
- Mile 15.5: Turn right onto Campground Road and reward yourself with post-ride relaxation in the shadow of Moore's Wall.

Pilot Knob Summit *4-mile out-and-back, 45 minutes–1 hour, strenuous, views of Pilot Mountain and the Yadkin River Valley, bragging rights*

If you're just looking for a short, but epic (in the most painful sense of the word) two-wheeled challenge, start at the Pilot Mountain Visitor Center and slog your way up Pilot Knob Park Road. It's just under 2 miles to the top, but, with an average grade of 9.2%, 2 miles will be enough. Celebrate your victory with views from the summit parking lot and get ready to fly back down to the visitor center. Even the most adventurous of moms would tell you to be extremely careful!

We only recommend doing this ride early in the morning, especially in the summer and fall, when the park road is bumper-to-bumper traffic. Plan to finish your Tour-de-Pilot by 9 a.m. at the latest.

Views from Moore's Knob

Directions From Hanging Rock State Park, turn left onto Moore's Springs Road and continue 5.4 miles. Turn left onto NC 66 South. At mile 4.9, turn right onto Chestnut Grove Road. After 3 miles, turn left to stay on Chestnut Grove Road. Continue 1.1 miles, then turn right onto NC Old 52. After 3.1 miles, turn left onto Old Winston Road. Continue 0.4 mile, then turn left onto Pilot Knob Park Road. Follow Pilot Knob Park Road to the visitor center.

Mount Airy Cyclery *144 W. Oak St., Mount Airy; 336-719-2453*

Part bike shop, part bike museum, with more than 70 vintage bikes on display. Don't be surprised if your quick stop for a spare tube turns into an hour (or several) of bike gawking. Closed on Sundays.

HIKING ●

Moore's Wall Loop (Hanging Rock) *5 miles, 2–3 hours, moderate, 360-degree views, fire tower, wildflowers, stream*

This hike is so close to the campground that you could almost roll out of your tent and onto the trail. OK, maybe it's not that close, but it's only a short stroll from any site.

Look for the trail sign between the two campground loops and head north on the red-blazed Moore's Wall Loop Trail. At mile 0.25, there's an easy creek crossing. Past the creek, head uphill on impressively huge stone steps. At mile 1.2, follow signs to the lookout tower. On your way there, make a quick side trip to Balanced Rock, a large boulder perched just so on top of another rock. Continue ahead to the Moore's Knob Observation Tower for 360-degree views of the Piedmont, the park lake, Pilot Mountain, and on clear days, the Blue Ridge Mountains. You're on top of the world here at 2,579 feet . . .

Moore's Wall Loop

or at least on top of the ancient Sauratown Mountains, as Moore's Knob is the tallest peak in the range.

Retrace your steps back to the Moore's Wall Loop Trail and follow the red blazes down the mountain, past the junction with Tory's Den (mile 2.7) to the blue-blazed Magnolia Springs Trail at mile 3.4. Here, you can continue on the Moore's Wall Loop Trail (now flat and smooth) back to the campground or follow the trail on the left for an easy out-and-back side trip to Magnolia Springs. The last time we hiked this loop, we ended up right back at our tent!

Mountain/Grindstone/Ledge Spring Loop (Pilot Mountain) *8-mile loop (10-mile option), 3–5 hours, moderate, cliffs, boulders, views*

It's easy to score great views from the Pilot Mountain summit parking lot. But we think that the park's trails are definitely worth exploring. Plus, because this hike starts at the visitor

On the trail to Pilot Mountain

center, you'll avoid the often maxed-out parking lot at the summit. Make a quick stop at the visitor center before you hike. It's tiny, but there's tons of great literature there. You'll find maps, of course, but there's also information on park geology, wildflowers, history, climbing and more. Grab some info, then head across the road to the trailheads for the Mountain and Grindstone Trails.

Turn left on the red-blazed Mountain Trail. At the junction with the Grassy Ridge Trail, head right to continue on the Mountain Trail. This section of trail is well groomed, with only gentle ups and downs—a perfect warm-up. Around mile 2, the trail becomes rockier, and shortly thereafter the surrounding forest begins to look rather sparse. In 2012 a controlled burn spread beyond the intended burn area, affecting about 675 acres of the park.

Around mile 3, look for two sets of boulders popular with climbers: the Feel Good and Feel Better boulders that hug both sides of the trail. These impressive boulders were named because they're so good that climbers will supposedly feel better about having to hike back uphill. Of course, you'll be ascending too, but it's easier going without a crash pad strapped to your back! At mile 4.1, the Mountain Trail ends. Turn right onto the blue-blazed Grindstone Trail. The Grindstone Trail is fairly steep here as you start your ascent to the Ledge Spring cliffs. At the Y-junction at mile 4.7, head left to follow the combined Grindstone/Ledge Spring Trail. In 0.5 mile, get your first taste of the cliffs. Continue along the top of the cliffs, stopping to soak in views of the Piedmont below. Most weekends, you can watch as climbers take advantage of the cliffs' numerous top-roping opportunities.

At this point, you have a few options. You can backtrack on the Grindstone/Ledge Spring Trail to the junction with the Mountain Trail to continue the loop on

the Grindstone Trail. Or, to check out the base of the cliffs without adding much mileage, shimmy your way down Three Bears Gully; steep steps in between cliffs lead down to the Ledge Spring Trail. Here, you can head right on the Ledge Spring Trail and backtrack to the Mountain Trail/Grindstone Trail junction. Or, if you want to check out the Pinnacles and don't mind adding an easy 2 miles to your route, continue past Three Bears Gully on the Grindstone/Ledge Spring Trail to the summit parking lot. Follow the sidewalk past the parking lot overlook, and then turn right on the spur trail, which ends at another overlook. Here, you can take in classic views of Big Pinnacle, that gigantic protrusion of rock topped with vegetation that Pilot Rock is most known for. Geology lesson: While Big Pinnacle looks like a giant chia pet, it's actually a metamorphic quartz monadnock—an isolated hill or mountain that rises from the relatively flat land around it.

From the overlook, follow the Jomeokee Trail to the right, continuing past the intersection with the yellow-blazed Ledge Spring Trail. Shortly after this junction, the Jomeokee Trail splits. Stay straight to make a clockwise 0.5-mile loop around the base of Big Pinnacle. The cliffs here are a national natural landmark, and climbing on them is not permitted. When you reach the Ledge Spring Trail again (yellow blazes), head left and follow the trail along the base of the cliffs back to the Grindstone Trail. No matter which route you choose, when you reach the junction of the Grindstone and Mountain Trails, continue right on the Grindstone Trail (blue blazes). In about 0.4 mile, pass a spur trail that leads to the campground. From here, it's an easy 1-mile stroll on the Grindstone Trail back to the visitor center.

Directions Follow directions to Pilot Mountain State Park on page 156.

CLIMBING ⊘

Pilot Rock *Single-pitch sport, trad, and top-rope routes, 5.4–5.12, easy access, beginner–advanced, southern exposure, climbers must register at top of crag or at park office, can be busy on weekends, best in fall, winter, and spring*

Top-ropers and novices rejoice! Most of the North Carolina climbing scene is limited to big-exposure, multi-pitch traditional-style climbing, but the cliffs along the southwestern flank of Pilot Mountain provide an excellent opportunity to introduce your friends and family to the joys of rock without the high price of entry that Moore's Wall demands. There are more than 70 recognized routes

Top of the rock at Pilot Mountain

along the base of the Ledge Spring Trail, roughly divided west to east by Three Bears Gully, your main access for top-rope anchors. Most routes here are top-roped with a handful of bolted lead climbs. Some have anchors drilled into the rock at the top of the cliff, while others necessitate using natural anchors. Pick up the free "Climber's Guide to Pilot Mountain State Park" at the visitor center or download it at carolinaclimbers.org. Little Amphitheater is a particularly good spot if your group has varied skill levels. Located just east of Three Bears Gully, this area has at least six good 5.5–5.8 routes. Most routes have bolts along the top of the cliff edge. Need motivation? The cliffs are only 5–10 minutes from the parking lot and we love the friendly atmosphere we always find here.

> **Directions** Follow directions to Pilot Mountain State Park on page 156. From the summit parking lot, take the Grindstone Trail west to the signed Three Bears Gully.

Moore's Wall *Multi-pitch trad climbing, 5.5–5.14, moderate–expert, northern exposure, best March–November, experience in traditional multi-pitch climbing or guide recommended, bouldering nearby, climbers must register at trailhead parking area*

Remember the views from the top of the Moore's Wall lookout tower? The mountain drops precipitously to the north and west to form the famously exposed cliffs of Moore's Wall. Whereas Pilot Mountain offers accessibility, Moore's Wall offers extreme exposure, massive height, and a much quieter climbing experience. This area has routes appealing to intermediate and expert climbers alike, and can be a great introduction to multi-pitch trad climbing if you bring a guide or a highly skilled friend. We recommend starting at the

■ Moore's Wall

Sentinel Buttress, the most prominent wall to the right of Moore's Wall, where you'll find a great mix of 1–3 pitch routes, ranging from 5.5 to 5.11. For detailed descriptions of the climbs, we recommend picking up a copy of Yon Lambert and Harrison Shull's book *Selected Climbs in North Carolina.*

Directions From Hanging Rock State Park, turn left onto Moore's Spring Road, then immediately turn left onto Hall Road. Take Hall Road for 2.8 miles, then turn left onto Mickey Road. After 0.8 mile, turn left onto Charlie Young Road. Follow Charlie Young Road for 0.5 mile, and then turn right onto Hooker Farm Road. In 0.5 mile, turn right onto Climbing Access Dr. Parking here is limited and camping is prohibited. Take the short access trail near the kiosk to a gravel road and turn left. When this road levels out, look for a trail on the right that leads up to the middle of the Central Wall; Sentinel Buttress is to the right. Before you reach the main wall, look for a trail on the right that leads to a boulder field. Most routes are within a mile of the parking lot. Check the kiosk or call the park for closure information, as Moore's Wall is a peregrine falcon nesting site.

Rock Dimensions *139 S. Depot St., Boone; 888-595-6009; rockdimensions.com*

Top-rope and multi-pitch guided climbing at Hanging Rock and Pilot. All gear provided. Even experienced climbers will appreciate their guide's insider knowledge of these areas.

■ Balanced Rock

PADDLING ⊗

For some easy flatwater paddle playtime, Hanging Rock State Park rents canoes and rowboats for use on the park's 12-acre lake for $5/hour. (Private boats not allowed.) The Yadkin River Canoe Trail runs through Pilot Mountain State Park, and park rangers occasionally offer guided canoe trips. Call or check their website for more information.

Dan River *12.85-mile run (6.5–mile option), Class I–II, 5–8 hours (depending on water levels), put in at Hart's Access, take out at Hanging Rock Access*

This is our go-to river in the Piedmont. If the water is up—which it usually is from spring to early summer—paddle the almost 13-mile section from Hart's Access to Hanging Rock Access, located on state park property. For the first 6.5 miles, you'll paddle almost nonstop Class I rapids through a thick corridor of trees. Around mile 5.5, navigate around a series of rock islands that create a Class II rapid when the water is up. At Clements Ford (mile 6), carefully maneuver through some shallow shoals. Pass under a bridge at mile 6.5; shortly after, Big Creek enters on river right. Here, the river widens as you paddle through the privately owned Hammer-Stern Wilderness Preserve. Within the next mile, both the North and South Forks of Double Creek enter on the right. The Saura Indians settled the fertile area between the two forks. Pass the Moore's Springs Campground, now closed, at mile 8.5, and enjoy a calm float. The Dan runs through Hanging Rock State Park for the last mile of your paddle. Here, stunning, steep rock cliffs known as the Dan River Bluffs loom above. Navigate the Play Wave Rapid just before the end of the bluffs, then watch for the Hanging Rock takeout on river right. We recommend self-shuttling with two cars or arranging a shuttle with the Dan River Company.

■ Dan River Bluffs

When the river is low, you can still do the last 6.5 miles of the run above by starting at Lynchburg Road Bridge, off of NC 89. Parking here is limited, however, and the put-in is steep and often muddy. We recommend arranging for an inexpensive shuttle with the Dan River Company, which has a private put-in just downriver of the bridge.

Directions to put-in From Hanging Rock State Park, turn left onto Piedmont Springs Road. After 0.9 mile, turn left onto NC 8 North/NC 89 West for 8.8 miles. Turn right onto NC 704 and continue 1.9 miles. There is an access road to the put-in just beyond the bridge. Ample parking is available.

Directions to takeout Hanging Rock State Park Dan River Access, 1258 Flinchum Road, Danbury. From Hanging Rock State Park, turn left onto Piedmont Springs Road. After 0.9 mile, turn left onto NC 8 North/NC 89 West. Continue 0.4 mile, then turn left onto Flinchum Road. Continue 0.3 mile. Ample parking is at the end of the road.

Dan River Company *1110 Flinchum Road, Danbury; 336-593-2628; danrivercompany.com*

Open April 1–October 31. Canoe/kayak rentals and shuttles on the hour 9 a.m.–1 p.m. (call for reservations). 6.2- and 13-mile trips; doggie lifejackets available. Located adjacent to the Green Heron Ale House.

VERTICAL ADVENTURES

Carolina Ziplines Canopy Tour *1085 Nickell Farm Road, Westfield; 336-972-7656; carolinaziplines.com*

One of the first canopy tours in the state, Carolina Ziplines offers something for just about everyone. Minimum age is 3. If your day is jam packed, check out the twilight zipline tour. Check website for prices and hours.

MAPS

No need to purchase maps for this weekend adventure. Free trail maps are available at both state parks and on their websites. A map for the Moore's Springs bike trails is available at the trailhead or at ncparks.gov/sites/default/files /ncparks/maps-and-brochures/hanging-rock-bike-trails.pdf. For a river access map, visit danriver.org.

RAINY DAY

Horne Creek Farm (NC Historic Site) *308 Horne Creek Farm Road, Pinnacle; 336-325-2298*

Think camping is roughing it? Imagine farm life in the early 20th century. Check out the original farmhouse, restored and furnished as it might have been more than a hundred years ago. There are also several other farm buildings, a visitor center and gift shop, and short trails on the property. Interpreters make history come alive some weekends. No fee. Closed Sundays and Mondays.

FOOD AND DRINK

Green Heron Ale House *1110 Flinchum Road, Danbury; 336-593-4733; greenheronalehouse.com*

Located next door to the Dan River Company and only 2 miles from Hanging Rock State Park, they have 20 taps and a riverside deck. Dirtbag and dog friendly, laid-back atmosphere, and music every Saturday night. Closed January–March; call or check website for hours.

■ Green Heron Ale House

Artist's Way Creations *508 Main St., Danbury; 336-593-2901; artistswaycreations.com*

Great place to grab a quick sandwich and sides for lunch. If you don't usually have dessert with your lunch, change your ways. The baked goods are ridiculously adorable and taste even better than they look. Closed Sundays and Mondays.

GEAR AND RESUPPLY

If you can't find what you need in town, head into Winston-Salem (45 minutes from Hanging Rock, 30 minutes from Pilot Mountain), where there's a Great Outdoor Provision Co. for all your outdoor gear needs.

Danbury General Store *201 North Main St., Danbury; 336-593-8780; danburygeneralstore.net*

Ten minutes from Hanging Rock State Park, this small but well-stocked convenience store has food staples, camping supplies, and even Carhartt gear, if you're in need of some sturdy clothing.

Robby's *457 North Main St., Mount Airy; 336-786-8017; shoprobbys.com*

Twenty minutes from Pilot Mountain, this is an easy stop if you've forgotten camping supplies. Make your way past the camouflage and ammunition and you'll find a decent selection of camping gear.

Sunset over Badin Lake

UWHARRIE NATIONAL FOREST

The Uwharrie Mountains, the oldest mountain range in North America, once loomed 20,000 feet high. While time and weather have eroded these peaks to their current 1,000-foot status, the Uwharrie National Forest is still a treasure trove of adventure. This remote area offers miles of hiking trails, including the 20-mile Uwharrie National Recreation Trail, lakeside camping, hidden cliffs and waterfalls, IMBA-designed mountain bike trails, and lake and river paddling. Plus, we weren't kidding about the treasure—the area was home to nearly 200 gold mines in the 19th century, so who knows? Maybe you'll go home with more than memories!

Areas included: Badin Lake, Birkhead Mountains Wilderness, Uwharrie River, Wood Run Mountain Bike Area, Yadkin River

Adventures: Camping, mountain biking, hiking, flatwater and whitewater paddling, gold mining

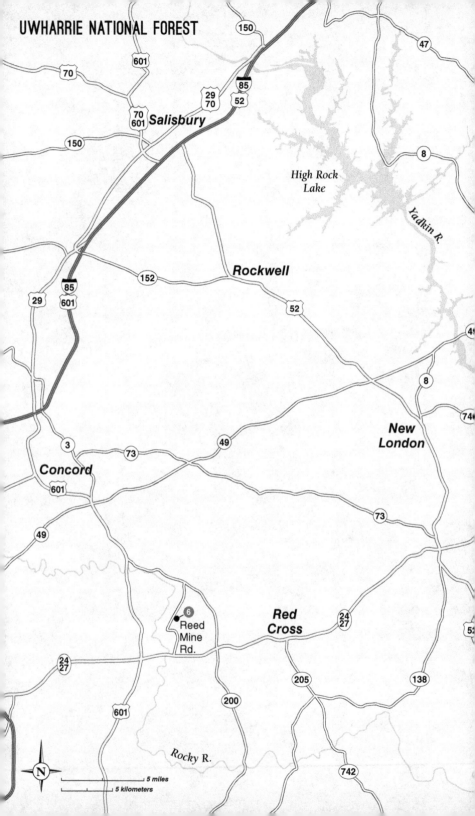

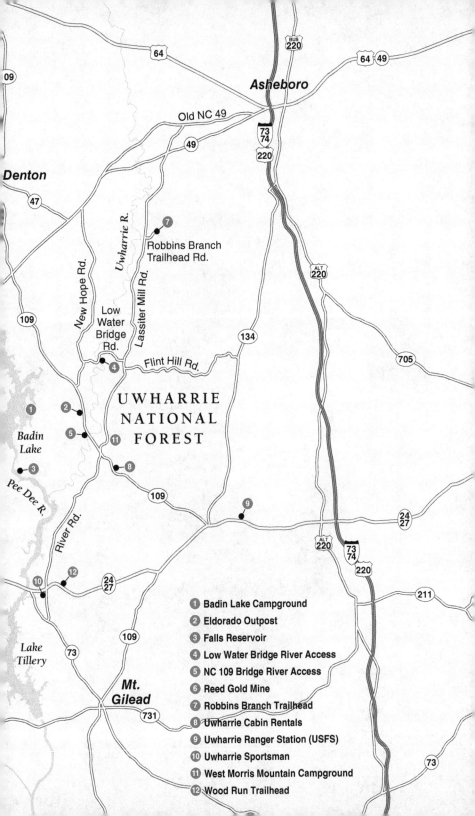

Asheboro

Old NC 49

Denton

Uwharrie R.

Robbins Branch
Trailhead Rd.

New Hope Rd.

Lassiter Mill Rd.

Low
Water
Bridge
Rd.

Flint Hill Rd.

UWHARRIE
NATIONAL
FOREST

*Badin
Lake*

Pee Dee R.

River Rd.

*Lake
Tillery*

**Mt.
Gilead**

1 Badin Lake Campground

2 Eldorado Outpost

3 Falls Reservoir

4 Low Water Bridge River Access

5 NC 109 Bridge River Access

6 Reed Gold Mine

7 Robbins Branch Trailhead

8 Uwharrie Cabin Rentals

9 Uwharrie Ranger Station (USFS)

10 Uwharrie Sportsman

11 West Morris Mountain Campground

12 Wood Run Trailhead

LODGING 🏕

TOP PICK

BADIN LAKE CAMPGROUND (USFS) *429 Badin Lake Recreation Area Road, Troy; 910-576-6391; www.fs.usda.gov. $12/night, open year-round, 34 sites, most sites can be reserved, picnic table, fire ring, tent pad, flush toilets, hot showers, shared water, no hookups*

■ A great way to end your day of Uwharrie adventure

You have your pick of campgrounds in the Uwharrie National Forest, but Badin Lake Campground, located on the eastern shore of its namesake lake, is our hands-down favorite. You can't beat having a spacious, wooded site that sits just above the lake, with paddling and hiking opportunities right outside of your tent door. Plus, the campground host does a great job of keeping the facilities spotless and in good repair.

The campground is divided into two loops. The upper loop is more wooded but farther from the lake than the lower loop. We stayed in the lower loop on our last Uwharrie weekend and could easily carry our boat to the water, where we spent hours exploring the wooded coves of Badin Lake. There are several short hikes easily accessible from all the campsites, so if your ideal weekend is full of hiking and paddling, you might never have to leave the campground!

Directions From Troy, take NC 109 North for 10 miles. Turn left onto FS 1154/Mullinax Road. After 1.6 miles, turn right onto FS 544/McLeans Creek Road. Travel for 1.7 miles, then turn right onto Badin Lake Road. After 0.2 mile, turn left and continue 1 mile to the campground.

■ Take a sunset paddle on Badin Lake.

West Morris Mountain Campground *600 Ophir Road, Troy; 910-576-6391; www.fs.usda.gov. $5/night, open year-round, 14 sites and 2 group sites, first come, first served, picnic table, fire ring, tent pad, lantern post, vault toilet, no showers or water, no hookups*

West Morris is an underutilized and rustic campground, ideal for tent campers who want to avoid camping in the shadow of large RVs. A short connector trail from the campsite leads to the 20-mile Uwharrie National Recreation Trail, making this a great launching pad for a weekend of hiking.

INDOOR LODGING

Uwharrie Cabin Rentals *2580 NC 109, Troy; 800-516-2309; uwharriecabins.com. $105– $350/night, twin, full, and queen beds, fully stocked kitchen, heat and air-conditioning, private bath, TV, grill, no pets*

The seclusion of the Uwharrie National Forest is great for outdoor adventures; not so much for creature comforts. Luckily, these locally owned and operated cabins, located on the Uwharrie's doorstep, are clean and cozy, have screened-in porches, and sleep 2–22. The Ponderosa Cabin is western-themed, in case you've been craving a chance to release your inner cowboy.

■ Uwharrie Mountain Range

MOUNTAIN BIKING

Wood Run/Keyauwee/Supertree Loop *13-mile loop, 1.5 hours, intermediate, 90% singletrack, creek crossings, rock gardens, fast and flowy*

The Wood Run Mountain Bike Trails offer 20 miles of fun, intermediate-level singletrack and many more miles of beginner-friendly forest roads. Bikers and hikers can get a lot of bang for their buck here, as the hiking-only Uwharrie and Dutchman's Creek Trails start from the same parking lot as the bike trails. These trails are regularly maintained by the Uwharrie SORBA, the Tarheel Trailblazers, and the Uwharrie Trails and Conservancy, and have been steadily growing and improving since their inception in 1998. The area was designated

■ View from Robbins Branch Loop

an IMBA Ride Center in 2007, and local trail advocates have received grants to add new and revitalized trails throughout the system.

Start at the Wood Run Trailhead on NC 24/27. All bike trails are blue-blazed; the white- and yellow-blazed trails in the area are for hikers only. Head past the gate on Wood Run Road. Ride for 0.5 mile, then turn right onto the 1.4-mile Wood Run Trail. You'll bounce through mini rock gardens, hit rollers, and carve through tree gauntlets as you navigate the east side of the ridge below Wood Run Road. The trail ends at Wood Run Camp, a primitive U.S. Forest Service campground with a vault toilet.

Cross the road and take the Keyauwee Trail (395A) for a 6-mile journey through the hills and streams of Uwharrie. Climb up and over Walker Mountain, getting a small taste for what these ancient hills were like when they were 20,000-foot giants. After Walker Mountain, relax on some rolling terrain, and then hold on tight as you fly down the most intense descent of the ride. Send out a cosmic thank-you to the trail builders for the beautiful berms, then get ready to pay your dues. After a tricky rock garden—we learned the hard way to veer left—you'll begin a steady 1.5-mile climb to the junction with Wood Run Road and the Supertree Trail. Go straight across Wood Run Road to start the Supertree Trail (doubletrack at this point), then turn left to stay on Supertree. Supertree is less technical than the Wood Run and Keyauwee Trails and ideal for less-experienced or tired-legged mountain bikers. Enjoy this roller coaster of a ride, with short climbs followed by wide-open, fast doubletrack downhills.

Follow Supertree back to Wood Run Camp, then veer left to take Wood Run Trail back to Wood Run Road and the parking lot.

> **Directions** From Badin Lake Campground, turn right onto FS 597A/Badin Lake Campground Road, then turn left onto FS 544/McLeans Creek Road. After 1.7 miles, turn left onto FS 1154 and continue 1.6 miles. Turn right onto NC 109 South. Travel for 3.1 miles, then turn right onto River Road. Continue 8.5 miles and turn left onto NC 24/27. The parking lot is 1.1 miles on the left.

BIKING NOTES

Mountain biking is permitted on some of the hiking trails in Uwharrie, but the only trails we found to be weekend-worthy for biking were the ones in the Wood Run Trail System.

Several bike shops have come and gone in this area, and there are currently no bike shops near the Uwharrie National Forest. Bring all the spare parts, tubes, and tools you need, and if possible, your most mechanically inclined buddy.

HIKING ☁

Robbins Branch Loop *6.7-mile loop, creeks, interesting rock formations, back-country campsites, evidence of past settlement, winter views*

The Birkhead Mountains Wilderness is the northernmost section of the once-majestic Uwharrie Mountains. It's our go-to place in Uwharrie to soak in views and imagine what this area was like when the mountains were towering beasts.

■ Birkhead Mountains Wilderness

This loop is a gentle hike, with a few sustained but manageable climbs. If you're trying to introduce your kids to hiking longer distances, this is a great practice hike. We've seen quite a few families with happy kiddos out on these trails. You'll get great winter views of the Birkhead and Uwharrie Mountains from the Birkhead Mountain Trail. Along Hannah's Creek, watch for rock walls and crumbling chimneys: evidence of 18th- and 19th-century settlements.

Park at the Robbins Branch Trailhead and start your hike on the Robbins Branch Trail, which meets the Hannah's Creek Trail at mile

0.3. Turn right onto Hannah's Creek Trail. Hike for 1.4 miles, then turn left at the junction with the Birkhead Mountain Trail. Follow the Birkhead Mountain Trail as it heads uphill and along the ridge of Coolers Knob Mountain. After 2 miles on the Birkhead Mountain Trail, turn left on the Robbins Branch Trail, following the trail down the side of the mountain. Hike alongside the trail's namesake drainage before turning uphill. Continue past the right-hand junction with the Thornburg Trail to follow a gentle ridge back to the trailhead.

Directions From Badin Lake Campground, turn right onto FS 597A/Badin Lake Campground Road, then turn right onto FS 597/Badin Lake Road. Take the first left onto McLeans Creek Road/FS 544. In 1.7 miles, turn left onto FS 1154/Mullinax Road. Continue 1.5 miles, then turn left onto NC 109. In 1 mile, turn right onto Coggins Mine Road and travel for 2.6 miles to Low Water Bridge Road. Turn right onto Low Water Bridge Road. After 3.1 miles, turn left onto Ophir Road (which becomes Burney Mill). Drive 3.2 miles, and then turn right onto Lassiter Mill Road. In 5 miles, look for the Robbins Branch Trailhead Road on the right. The trailhead is at the end of a short gravel road.

Dutchman's Creek/Uwharrie Loop *12-mile loop, moderate terrain, creeks, ridges, rhododendron and hardwood forest, close to mountain biking*

Dutchman's Creek Trail and Uwharrie National Recreation Trail both start at the Wood Run Trailhead off of NC 24/27 in the southwestern quadrant of Uwharrie National Forest. The Uwharrie NRT is a 20-mile, point-to-point trail. Dutchman's Creek is an 11.2-mile point-to-point trail as well, and the trails intersect 6 miles from the trailhead, affording hikers a great loop hike without fear of being run over by the mountain bikers who share this area. (No bikes are allowed on Dutchman's Creek and the Uwharrie NRT.) This is not a hike for basking in great views; instead, it's a way to get in some Zen trail miles through a peaceful, hardwood forest.

Start the Dutchman's Creek Trail (yellow blazes) from the east side of the Wood Run parking lot. Cross a footbridge at mile 0.3, and then follow the rolling terrain up and down, up and down, up and down . . . and then down some more as you cross another creek. Continue to follow the yellow blazes as you cross the Supertree Trail (watch for bikers) and, a mile later, the Whitetail Trail. You'll cross over Wood Run Road (again, bikers!), then reach Big Island Creek at mile 5.2. There's a nice campsite here that also makes a good snack or hammock stop (it is the weekend, after all). At mile 6, turn left onto the Uwharrie NRT. You'll cross Big Island Creek and several small streams, and then you'll intersect the Keyauwee Trail at mile 7.9. Crest Dennis Mountain, then it's easy hiking back to the trailhead, with a few more stream crossings thrown in for good measure.

Directions Follow directions to the Wood Run Mountain Bike Area in the biking section on page 171.

🙂 Badin Lake Trail Loop

5.2-mile loop, 2.5 hours, easy,
lake views, creekside hiking, bluffs,
freshwater clams, bird-watching

We're suckers for a good lake hike. And a waterside hike that starts from our campsite? You're speaking our language. We won't claim that the Badin Lake Trail Loop is our favorite Uwharrie trail. It's a bit overhiked, and you could definitely show it some trail love by bringing a trash bag to pack out litter. But the trail makes up for its weaknesses in other ways. There are plenty of opportunities to watch for great blue herons, ospreys, and even bald eagles. Wander down to the lakeshore and you might find freshwater clams. While we certainly wouldn't call this trail technical, you will come across rocky sections. Watch for lakeside rocky outcrops, perfect for a pit stop, and quartz slabs that look a bit like chunks of ice.

■ Badin Lake Trail

From Badin Lake Campground, find the white-blazed Badin Lake Trail behind the lakeside sites on the lower loop. Facing the lake, turn right onto the trail to start your clockwise loop. After 1 mile of lakeside hiking, you'll reach the Kings Mountain Picnic Area, where there's a fishing pier, dock, and disc golf course. Cut across the parking lot and continue along the trail for 0.9 mile to Kings Mountain Point, a peninsula popular with fishermen (and fisherwomen).

Continue around the other side of the point, leaving the lake (for now). You'll soon come to a small, picturesque creek lined with pine, oak, cedar, and holly trees and, when it's warm, wildflowers. Enjoy—or endure—some mild hills as you leave the lakeshore. Around mile 4.5, cross a gravel road and then join the Josh Trail (green blazes). Continue to follow the white blazes as you continue past the junction with the Lake Horse Trail (more green blazes). Shortly after, cross another gravel road and follow the (now paved) trail to the Arrowhead Campground. The trail makes a figure eight around the campground, which is not as tent friendly or as scenic as the Badin Lake Campground in our opinion. To continue on your loop, keep the lake on your left and head back to Badin Lake Campground.

Uwharrie River

PADDLING ⊗

WHITEWATER

Uwharrie River *7 miles, 3–4 hours, Class I+ whitewater, check water levels before paddling, put in at Low Water Bridge, take out under the NC 109 bridge*

The Uwharrie River is a remote and scenic float through the past. You won't see much recent development along this stretch—much of the surrounding land is national forest or protected by the Land Trust for Central North Carolina—but you will paddle past the remains of old bridges, mills, and even gold mines. The first documented gold in the United States was found in this area in 1799, so we won't blame you if you stop for a bit of treasure hunting. Most of the time, this stretch runs shallow and even first-time paddlers can easily cruise along. Fallen trees will be your biggest challenge, so be especially careful in early spring and after storms, when strainers clog the waterway. Watch for great blue herons, bald eagles, deer, wild turkeys, and, if you hit the wildlife jackpot, river otters.

Just before the NC 109 bridge (the only bridge on this section), Barnes Creek enters on the left. If the water is up, you can paddle upstream here. The takeout is under the NC 109 bridge on the right, and it's a short but steep climb to the parking lot. If there's been recent significant rainfall, you can do a 15-mile paddle from Low Water Bridge to Morrow Mountain State Park in 6–7 hours. However, we don't recommend attempting it if the water isn't flowing fast, unless you're ready for a long day in the boat!

Shuttles are available from El Dorado Outpost for $10; just call to arrange your ride. Adventurous paddlers can self-shuttle with a bike. There's ample parking but no bathrooms at the put-in and takeout. Check water levels before you put in, as Low Water Bridge's name is no exaggeration. This section is usually runnable until early summer; after that, you'll want to stick to lake paddling. There are no gauges on the river, but if you call El Dorado Outpost they can give you river beta. You can also rent kayaks or canoes from the Outpost.

> **Directions to put-in** From Badin Lake Campground, turn right onto FS 597A/Badin Lake Campground Road, then turn right onto Badin Lake Road. Turn left onto FS 544/McLeans Creek Road. Continue 1.7 miles, then turn left onto FS 1154. After 1.6 miles, turn left onto NC 109 North and travel for 1 mile. Turn right onto Coggins Mine Road. Drive 1.6 miles, and then turn right onto Low Water Bridge Road. Put-in is 1.1 miles down the road.

> **Directions to takeout** From Low Water Bridge, head southwest, then turn left onto Coggins Mine Road. Continue 1.6 miles, then turn left onto NC 109 South. Takeout is 2.7 miles on the right.

FLATWATER

Badin Lake If you're lucky enough to snag a lakeside site at Badin Lake Campground, you can launch your craft onto Badin Lake and explore the lake's peaceful coves. This man-made impoundment of the Yadkin River is a birder's paradise, so paddle quietly to increase your chances of sighting a bald eagle, hooded warbler, scarlet tanager, or other migrating waterfowl. Motorboat traffic subsides in the evenings and this is actually our favorite time to paddle on the lake (with adequate lights, of course). You can also access the lake from the Cove Boat Launch, located 0.5 mile past the entrance to the Arrowhead Campground, south from Badin Lake Campground on FS 597B.

■ Low Water Bridge on the Uwharrie River

Falls Reservoir Craving solitude? If you have a four-wheel-drive vehicle (and know how to use it), take your canoe or kayak to the Deep Water Boat Launch, located at the southern terminus of FS 576. The "road" down to the boat launch, past the primitive Deep Water Campground, is very steep, rough, and rocky. If your car isn't as adventurous as you are, park at the top of the hill in the camping area and carefully walk your boat about 0.25 mile to the water. You'll be rewarded for your treacherous journey.

Falls Reservoir

The reservoir is a paddler's playground with no lakeside development, deep coves, and rocky islands. From the launch area, we recommend paddling north (right) toward the dam, located about a mile up the reservoir. Bald eagle nests have been found along the shore here, so keep your eyes peeled. Use caution as you approach the dam, as water releases can create a solid stretch of Class II rapids in the deep Yadkin River. Hug the shoreline and the whitewater is easily avoidable. This area of the Yadkin was known as the Yadkin Narrows before Alcoa dammed it to create Badin Lake, Falls Reservoir, and Lake Tillery. Many paddlers reminisce about the pre-dam paddling here, claiming it was some of the best whitewater in North Carolina. It is also one of the deepest sections you'll paddle, with water depths up to 200 feet in some areas. On the way back, hug the northeast (left) shore to explore steep cliffs and waterfalls tucked into deep coves.

> *Directions* From Badin Lake Campground, turn right onto FS 597A/Badin Lake Campground Road, then turn right onto FS 597/Badin Lake Road. Follow FS 597 for 1.3 miles to FS 576/Moccasin Creek Road. Turn right on FS 576 and travel for 4.4 miles. Turn right at signs for Deep Water Trail Camp. Lake access is about 0.25 mile past the camp.

For outfitter information, check out Eldorado Outpost on page 177.

MAPS

Birkhead Mountains Wilderness Download a trail map at heartofnorthcarolina.com/travel-tools/images/Birkhead-Mountain-Wilderness.pdf.

Uwharrie National Forest Map and general information at www.fs.usda.gov /Internet/FSE_DOCUMENTS/stelprd3806290.pdf.

Wood Run Mountain Bike and Hiking Trails Overview maps at tarheeltrailblazers .com/trailmaps/uwharrie.pdf and also www.fs.usda.gov/Internet/FSE_DOCU MENTS/stelprdb5378693.pdf.

RAINY DAY 😊

Reed Gold Mine (NC Historic Site) *9621 Reed Mine Road, Midland; 704-721-4653; nchistoricsites.org/reed/reed.htm; free admission, closed Sundays and Mondays*

This isn't your typical "pan fer gold" tourist trap. Reed Gold Mine was the site of the first documented gold find in the United States (a 17-pound rock!). Now you can explore the restored underground tunnels, the stamp mill, and a small museum in the visitor center. And, yes, if the clouds clear, you can pan for gold from April 1–October 31. Know that the mine is almost 1 hour away from Badin Lake Campground.

FOOD AND DRINK 🥤

Uwharrie Sportsman *4593 NC 24/27 West, Mount Gilead; 910-439-4336*

Sometimes the call of nature takes you behind a large tree . . . and sometimes it tells you to stop and grab an ice-cream cone, a basket of fried anything, and maybe even an antique bobble or two. Lucky for you, you'll find all of these at Uwharrie Sportsman. It's only a mile from the Wood Run Trailhead, where you've probably burnt a few calories out on the trails. A double mint-chocolate chip cone will give you just the boost you need to get back to the campground after a solid day in the woods.

GEAR AND RESUPPLY 🛒

Eldorado Outpost *4021 NC 109 North, Troy; 910-572-3474; eldoradooutpost.com*

Don't think you need any supplies? Think of something you could use just for an excuse to check out this eclectic catchall of a country store. Beyond the jam-packed aisles of hunting, fishing, and camping gear; guidebooks; dry goods; candy you may have forgotten existed; and every flavor of soda, you'll also find a wealth of information about the area, if you're willing to ask and listen. On our last visit, a white-haired woman was playing hymns on the organ in the back while her audience watched from doily-covered antique tables, enjoying lunch and a quiet sing-along. This place is an adventure in itself. Eldorado also offers kayak trips down the Uwharrie River, shuttle service, and just about any typical Southern cuisine a hungry adventurer could want.

Paddle to Masonboro Island

WILMINGTON– CAROLINA BEACH

Like your adventure with a side of cool, classic beach town? You'll love this Carolina Beach trip. Camp at Carolina Beach State Park and go on a carnivorous plant scavenger hunt. You can't take the Venus flytraps with you, but you can paddle to Sharks Tooth Island and find, appropriately, a souvenir shark's tooth. Take a two-wheeled spin to get morning coffee in Wilmington or hit up the buff mountain bike trails at Blue Clay Bike Park. Get a dose of history with your hike at Fort Fischer Recreation Area and find some of the best surfing that the North Carolina coast has to offer on nearby Wrightsville Beach.

Areas included: Blue Clay Bike Park, Cape Fear River Basin, Fort Fisher Recreational Area, Freeman Park, Masonboro Island Reserve, Zeke's Island National Estuarine Research Reserve, Wrightsville Beach

Adventures: Camping, mountain and road biking, hiking, paddling, surfing

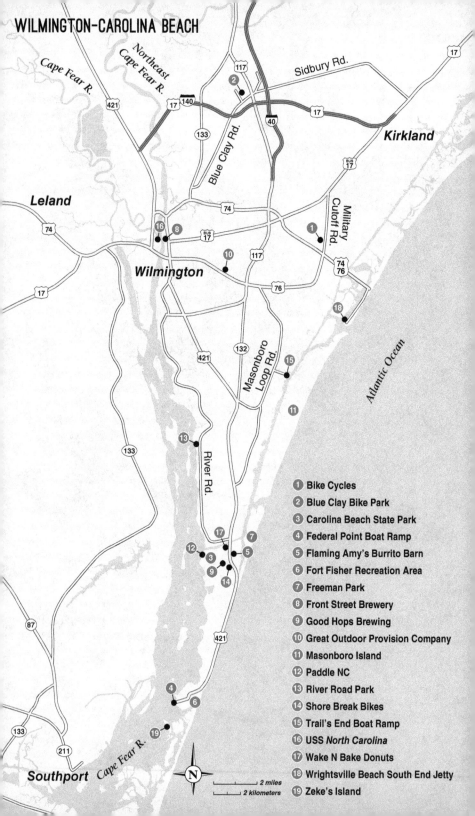

WILMINGTON–CAROLINA BEACH

Cape Fear R.

Northeast Cape Fear R.

Sidbury Rd.

117

17 140

40

133

Blue Clay Rd.

74

Kirkland

Leland

74

BUS 17

17

Military Cutoff Rd.

117

Wilmington

76

74 76

132

Masonboro Loop Rd.

421

River Rd.

133

87

421

133

211

Cape Fear R.

Southport

Atlantic Ocean

N

2 miles
2 kilometers

1 Bike Cycles
2 Blue Clay Bike Park
3 Carolina Beach State Park
4 Federal Point Boat Ramp
5 Flaming Amy's Burrito Barn
6 Fort Fisher Recreation Area
7 Freeman Park
8 Front Street Brewery
9 Good Hops Brewing
10 Great Outdoor Provision Company
11 Masonboro Island
12 Paddle NC
13 River Road Park
14 Shore Break Bikes
15 Trail's End Boat Ramp
16 USS *North Carolina*
17 Wake N Bake Donuts
18 Wrightsville Beach South End Jetty
19 Zeke's Island

TOP PICK

CAROLINA BEACH STATE PARK (NC STATE PARKS) *1010 State Park Road, Carolina Beach; 910-458-8206; ncparks.gov/carolina-beach-state-park. $20/night on weekends, open year-round, 83 sites, reservations accepted, picnic table, fire ring, flush toilets, hot showers, central water, electric sites available for $30/night*

This beach base camp is the best of both worlds. It's only a 5-minute drive to the shores of Carolina Beach, but you'll enjoy the sun and wind protection of towering longleaf pine and live oak trees that you don't get with beachfront camping. The sites are huge, especially the ones on the outside of the loops, so even when the campground is full, you won't feel like you're camping on top of your neighbors.

We prefer the back loop (sites 44 and up). If you're lucky enough to have your choice of sites, snag site 65 or 75. These sites are awesomely big, and you'll be able to tuck your tent way back in the woods.

The campground marina store sells essentials (bug spray and ice cold drinks, anyone?), and it's also a fun place to ogle cool boats and stargaze from the docks. There are 7 miles of trails in the park, most of which are easily accessible from the campground.

The visitor center is definitely worth a stop, with lots of hands-on activities and cool displays. If you're into carnivorous plants—and, really, who isn't?—the park is home to five different kinds, including the Venus flytrap. (In fact, the plant is only found within a 60- to 70-mile radius of this area. Did we hear a "Feed me, Seymour?") Gates are locked at night, so plan accordingly.

Directions *From the north and west* Follow I-40 East until it becomes NC 132. Continue south on NC 132 through Wilmington. When US 421 joins NC 132, continue south on US 421. After 6.5 miles, turn right onto Dow Road. In 0.3 mile, turn right onto Carolina Beach State Park Road.

From the south From I-74/US 74 East, follow US 74 to Wilmington. After crossing the Cape Fear River, take the exit for State Port onto US 421. Once on US 421, follow directions above.

Freeman Park (Town of Carolina Beach) *1800 Canal Dr., Carolina Beach; 910-458-4614; carolinabeach.org/visitors/freeman_park/freeman_park_camping.php. $10/night April–September plus $30 daily permit fee ($50 on holidays), open year-round, 119 sites, reservations accepted, portable toilets, no water, showers, or electricity, on-the-beach camping*

Ever dream about camping right on the beach? Then Freeman Park will make your wildest dreams come true . . . but you have to be up for the wild part, at least during the high season. You can drive on the beach here, and beer and wine are permitted. Know that the sites are right on top of one another, so hope you love your neighbor! (Of course, you can come in the off-season and avoid the crowds.) Trash must be packed out and fires must be contained, so bring a fire pit or fire pan.

INDOOR LODGING

Carolina Beach State Park Camping Cabins *1010 State Park Road, Carolina Beach; 910-458-8206; ncparks.gov/carolina-beach-state-park. $58/night, one double bed and two sets of bunk beds, heat and air-conditioning, picnic table, charcoal grills, fire ring, central water and shared bathrooms, no pets*

These cute little cabins are clean, climate-controlled, and the perfect place to practice tiny-house living. Bring linens and know that you'll be cooking alfresco or dining out, but you can't beat the price for a cozy place to crash after a day's adventures.

BIKING

MOUNTAIN BIKING

Blue Clay Bike Park *6-mile loop, 45 minutes, beginner–intermediate, jumps, berms, pump track*

Thanks to local volunteer efforts (Cape Fear SORBA, you rock!), these former bandit trails are beautifully constructed and have flow for days. (History buffs: the trails were built partially on the site of a 19th-century landfill near the county jail.)

To start the intermediate 6-mile loop, head left at the signed trailhead and follow the blue

Blue Clay Bike Park

trail signs. New riders or kids can veer right for the flat and remarkably smooth 1.5-mile beginner trail. Both loops are well signed, so there's no getting lost here. Some sections are nonstop twists and turns—typical of trails built in a limited space—but you won't get bored. There's always a fun feature ahead: a jump, bridge, punchy incline, or tight squeeze between some trees.

Blue Clay bridge

The first half of the trail winds through wetlands, but pavers and bridges prevent your tires from getting bogged down. At mile 3, you'll cross over Juvenile Center Road. Continue straight across to the "hilly side," which does have decent elevation change, at least for coastal riding. (We guess mountains of trash can be good for something.) At mile 5.8, cross back over the road for the last 0.25 mile to the parking lot. There is a pump track to the right of the parking lot, but it's seen, well, pumpier days. Check blog.capefearsorba.com for closures, especially after it rains.

Directions From Carolina Beach State Park, turn left onto Dow Road. After 0.2 mile, turn left onto US 421 North/North Lake Park Blvd. After 6.5 miles, continue straight onto South College Road, then follow South College Road/NC 132 North for 9.6 miles. Take Exit 420B to merge onto NC 132 North. After 3.3 miles, turn left onto Blue Clay Road for 0.5 mile, then turn right onto Juvenile Center Road. The park is on the right.

ROAD BIKING

Cape Fear River Ride *39 miles, 2.5 hours, easy–moderate, Cape Fear River views, ride from campsite, downtown Wilmington, coffee shop, USS North Carolina*

Starting at Carolina Beach State Park, exit the campground and turn left onto US 421. At mile 3, carefully cross the Intracoastal Waterway. Turn left onto River Road. At mile 16, turn right onto Shipyard Blvd., then immediately turn left onto Burnett Blvd. At mile 17.6, take a slight left onto South Front St. Follow South Front St. to North Front St. (past the intersection with Market St.). Stop for coffee and fresh baked goodies at Port City Java on your left. Continue north and turn left onto Princess St., which will bring you to a riverfront park and a view of the World War II–era battleship the USS *North Carolina*. Follow N. Water St. south along the river to Ann St. Turn left onto Ann St., then right back onto S. Front St. Retrace your route back to Carolina Beach State Park.

Shore Break Bikes *915 N. Lake Park Blvd., Carolina Beach; 910-880-1013; shorebreakbikes.com*

Need a tube, quick repair, or a rental cruiser? This shop is only 2 minutes from Carolina Beach State Park, so you can get back on two wheels fast.

Bike Cycles *6801 Parker Farm Road, Wilmington; 910-256-2545; bikecycleshop.com*

This full-service store will be become your bike shop home away from home. You'll leave happy and with everything you need. Open on Saturdays and Sundays too.

HIKING ☁

👥 Fort Fisher Recreation Area Basin Trail *2.2-mile out-and-back, 45 minutes, easy, dune hiking, boardwalks, WWII-era bunker, observation deck*

Even a lot of regular visitors to the Fort Fisher Recreation Area don't know this trail exists, which seems appropriate for a trail that leads to a World War II bunker that became the refuge of Robert E. Harrill, the Fort Fisher Hermit. Harrill

■ Boardwalk at Fort Fisher Recreation Area

lived in self-inflicted exile 1955–1972, becoming a folk hero to those who admired his self-sufficient and spartan lifestyle. (Ironically, this self-proclaimed hermit was the second most popular tourist attraction in North Carolina for a period of time.) Not a history buff? This stroll is still adventure weekend–worthy because of the amazing views and wildlife observation opportunities.

From the parking lot, head south past the bathrooms, just to the right of the visitor center. The trail starts in a (sometimes buggy) maritime forest, and then quickly opens up behind a gorgeous stretch of dunes. Long boardwalks provide an elevated view of the marsh and its inhabitants and also help to keep your shoes marsh mud-free.

This is a bird-watcher's paradise, as 200-plus species of birds visit the recreation area. Kids—and some adults (like us)—will enjoy the scavenger hunt challenge found on one of the interpretive signs; we managed to check fiddler crabs and snowy egrets off of our

Fort Fisher Basin Trail

list. A dilapidated stone WWII bunker comes into view at mile 0.8. It's a stark juxtaposition with the picture-perfect scenery you've been hiking through, but interesting in its own claustrophobia-inducing way. Continue past the bunker for 0.3 mile to an observation deck that offers views of the Cape Fear River, Zeke's Island, and windsurfers playing on the water. Return the way you came. If you're interested, there's also a North Carolina Aquarium at Fort Fisher.

Directions From Carolina Beach State Park, turn right onto Dow Road and continue 3.2 miles. Dow Road veers to the left and becomes K Ave. Continue 0.5 mile, then turn right onto US 421 South/Fort Fisher Blvd. for 2.3 miles. Turn left onto Loggerhead Road, then left into the parking area.

Sugarloaf Trail and Flytrap Trail Loop

5-mile loop, 2–3 hours, easy, tidal marsh, boardwalks, carnivorous plants, Cape Fear River views, mountainous sand dunes, Civil War history, maps available at the marina

This loop is a fun straight-from-your-campsite hike and also makes a great trail run—as long as you don't mind some sand in your shoes! Head toward site 54 and hop on the Campground Trail, blazed with blue circles. Follow this mile-long trail to its junction with the orange-blazed Sugarloaf Trail. Turn left to make a clockwise loop on the Sugarloaf Trail.

The terrain changes here, as the park does controlled burns in this area to ensure that native species can continue to grow and thrive. It's not the most scenic part of your hike and it's very exposed, but it's interesting to see the forest in a state of regrowth. You'll also encounter stretches of thick, calf muscle–enhancing sand along this stretch. We promise it gets easier! At mile 2.5, climb a hill (!) to the top of the 50-foot Sugarloaf Dune, used both as a navigational tool by boat captains and a line of defense for Confederate soldiers protecting the port of Wilmington. Picture 50,000 troops camping out here, then take in a bird's-eye view of the soundlike expanse of the Cape Fear River below. Head downhill, past the Oak Toe Trail on your left. Past the marina, continue left at the junction with the Swamp Trail until you reach the parking area on the right for the Flytrap Trail.

The marshy shores of the Cape Fear River

This 0.3-mile trail (blazed with orange diamonds) is a fun side trip through pocosin wetlands, savanna, swamp, and sand ridge. There's little tree canopy to provide shade, so a summer afternoon might not be the best time to hike, especially because you'll want to take your time looking for all the carnivorous plants that live here. Don't worry: the Venus flytraps, pitcher plants, sundews, and bladderworts won't jump up to bite you. Just the opposite, in fact; the tiny Venus flytraps are especially elusive, so put aside any *Little Shop of Horrors* visions. After finishing the loop, head back across the road to continue on the Sugarloaf Trail to the campground entrance.

■ Venus flytrap

PADDLING ⊗

Zeke's Island *2-plus miles, put in at Federal Point Boat Ramp, protected lagoon, shorebird habitat, island exploration*

Paddling across the Cape Fear River Basin (often referred to as the Basin) is a great excursion for beginner and intermediate paddlers. From the sandy kayak launch, you'll see Zeke's Island straight ahead. The 1,635-acre Zeke's Island National Estuarine Research Reserve is an East Coast hot spot for shorebirds, so bring binoculars and a camera.

The Basin is protected from the Cape Fear River to the west by a substantial rock seawall built by the U.S. Army Corps of Engineers, mitigating any fears of being swept out to the open river. And, even when the parking lot is full, motorized boat traffic in the basin is minimal. (Watch out for windsurfers, though!) Do keep in mind that water conditions here are affected by tides and coastal wind conditions can change in an instant, so use good judgment. No paddle is amazing enough to warrant putting yourself into a dangerous situation!

■ Zeke's Island

From Federal Point, it's a 1-mile straight shot across the basin to Zeke's, where you'll find stretches of sandy shore just right for parking a few kayaks. There aren't official hiking trails on the island, but you can easily explore the shrub thicket, dunes, and maritime forest via unofficial foot trails. This protected lagoon serves as a nursery for shrimp, fish, and crabs, so take the time to explore the marshy shoreline.

For another paddling adventure, head to the terminus of the Basin Trail. To spot it, look back at the kayak launch across the basin. To your left, you'll see the breakwater known as The Rocks, and to the right you'll see the grassy shoreline. Scan to the right along the shore and you'll find the end of the Basin Trail and a small observation deck. There's no official kayak launch here, but you can carefully finagle your way up to the trail and hike 0.3 mile to the WWII bunker.

Directions to put-in From Carolina Beach State Park, turn right onto Dow Road and continue 3.2 miles. Dow Road veers to the left and becomes K Ave. Continue 0.5 mile, then turn right onto US 421 South/Fort Fisher Blvd. Follow US 421 for 3.7 miles. The road ends in the parking area.

Masonboro Island Reserve *6-plus-mile out-and-back, put in at Trail's End Boat Ramp, pristine barrier island, diverse ecosystems, large, sandy beaches, island exploring, swimming*

Even though Masonboro Island is only accessible by boat, this 8.4-mile undeveloped barrier island still attracts a lot of beach lovers who want to escape the Wrightsville Beach crowds. Even on peak summer days, though, you'll always be able to find your own sandy stretch of paradise. However, there's so much to explore that you won't want to lounge on that beach chair for too long.

Follow the sandy shoreline or the island's inner footpaths, and you'll not only escape the crowds, you'll find creatures of all kinds. The translucent, nutrient-rich water is a nursery for numerous kinds of fish, so it's fun to explore in the shallow water. Within 5 minutes of a shoreline stroll, we found ghost and blue crabs, several orange-and-purple-hued starfish, and four huge conch shells. Keep your eyes peeled for shark's teeth and sea glass too. Masonboro is also home to seabeach amaranth, an endangered plant, and dozens of shorebirds nest here.

Be respectful of the island's flora and fauna: stick to established paths, avoid walking in the dunes, and set up beach chairs and umbrellas only in durable areas. There's no restroom facility or potable water on the island, and you'll need to pack out any trash that you (or any litterbugs) generate.

Start your paddle at the Trail's End Boat Ramp. There's a double-sided kayak launch to the left of the boat ramp. Avoid low tide, as the area around the launch becomes a giant mud flat. The entrance to the lagoon is on the other side of the launch, across the Intracoastal Waterway. Bring your best paddle game, as you'll share the waterway with boats that could eat a kayak for breakfast. (Most

■ Kayak landing, Masonboro Island

boaters are respectful of smaller crafts, but you'll still need to be aware of your surroundings while paddling.)

If you can, leave early on Saturday morning or paddle on Sunday, when there's less motorized boat traffic. Cross the waterway when safe to do so, then turn left to head northeast, past the lagoon entrance. Stay close to the right shore. At mile 2, turn right out of the Intracoastal into the Masonboro Channel. Paddle northeast in the channel for 1 mile, heading toward the sandy expanses of Masonboro's northwest shores. Pull up on the shoreline to the right, where you can arrange your beach chairs or follow the footpaths that lead up and over the dunes to the island's beach. Or, continue paddling northeast, turning east through the Masonboro Inlet (Wrightsville Beach will be on your left) and continue around the north tip of the island. Turn southwest along the shore, park on the beach, and enjoy a quieter side of Masonboro. Be aware of tidal and weather conditions, as you won't find shelter from a storm anywhere on the island. Return to the launch the way you came.

Directions to put-in From Carolina Beach State Park, turn left onto Dow Road Dr. for 0.2 mile, and then turn left onto US 421 North/North Lake Park Blvd. Follow US 421 North for 2.9 miles. Turn right onto Myrtle Grove Road. Continue 3.6 miles, then turn right onto Masonboro Loop Road. After 1.6 miles, turn right onto Trails End Road. The parking area is 0.5 mile on the left.

Sharks Tooth Island and Keg Island *1.5-plus-mile out-and-back, put in at River Road Park, shark tooth and fossil hunting*

Want to entice the kids (or reluctant friends) into going paddling? Make your destination a treasure hunt! Sharks Tooth and Keg Islands are the result of dredging on the lower Cape Fear River. The former is loaded with fossilized shark's teeth, whalebones, shells, and the occasional man-made oddity. (Funny stuff ends up on the bottom of rivers.)

From the put-in at River Road Park, which has ample parking and bathrooms, you'll see several barrier islands across the river. Keg Island is directly ahead. Sharks Tooth Island lines up with a light tower and is located at approximately two o'clock from the end of the boat ramp. You'll see the kayak and ferry tours that frequent the sandy beach on the island's tip.

If it looks crowded, don't panic. Head counterclockwise around the island, as few people explore past that initial stretch of beach. It's easy to circumnavigate this small island by kayak, and if you want a longer paddle, check out Keg Island.

From Sharks Tooth, Keg Island is the next island downstream (south). In the 2-mile paddle around Keg Island, you'll experience the island's transition from seagrass-festooned marshland to an elevated pine forest on the opposite side. If you're not up for that commitment (again, kids, reluctant friends, and so on), it's also fun to explore the small inlets through the marsh around Keg Island. If you choose to take a treasure home, choose one and leave the rest for others to discover, and grab any trash you see while you're at it, as all good pirates do.

Directions to put-in From Carolina Beach State Park, turn left onto Dow Road. Drive 0.2 mile, then turn left onto US 421 North/North Lake Park Blvd. After 1.2 miles, turn left onto River Road. Continue on River Road for 5.6 miles. River Road Park is on the left.

Mahanaim Adventures 910-547-8252, mahanaimadventures.com

No official address—they come to you. Canoe and kayak rentals, guided half- and full-day trips, and shuttle services. This family-run outfitter offers personalized service and caters to all kayakers, especially beginners.

Paddle NC 1010 State Park Road, Carolina Beach; 910-612-3297; paddlenc.com

Check out its Carolina Beach State Park location for kayak and SUP rentals, instruction, and tours, both in the park and off-site. Its 2-hour sunset tour is the perfect, not-too-strenuous end to a day of adventures. Reservations required; closed November–March, except by appointment.

Sharks Tooth Island

SURFING

As with most of the North Carolina coast, the best surf spots in this area change daily. The sand is always shifting, bringing awesome surf conditions to a spot one day and taking them away the next. We recommend hitting up Wrightsville Beach for your surf fix.

Stop by Surf City (530 Causeway Dr., Wrightsville Beach; 910-256-2265) if you want to talk surf and get current conditions. If you're a newbie, take a lesson with Sean's Private Surf Instruction (910-470-2010), just across the parking lot from Surf City. You'll get a one-on-one lesson with local instructors who really know their stuff.

Want to wing it? Here are your best bets for consistent breaks. Keep in mind that conditions are best August–October.

South End Jetty, Wrightsville Beach At the end of the causeway at Wrightsville Beach, turn right onto Waynick Blvd. Continue about 1 mile and park as far south as you can at one of the pay meters. Keep in mind that surfing is not allowed within 100 feet of the jetty or in front of the lifeguard stands from Memorial Day to Labor Day.

Masonboro Island If you're a strong and experienced surfer, and don't mind paddling for 20 minutes or so (or have a boat that can handle toting your board), check out the surf at Masonboro Island. Follow directions to the South End Jetty. From the beach, head past the gazebo and look straight out across the water, where you'll see Masonboro Island. Keep in mind that you'll be paddling back after you've caught enough waves, so save some energy.

MAPS

Cape Fear River NOAA's *Booklet Chart: New River Inlet to Cape Fear.* Available to download and print at charts.noaa.gov/BookletChart/11539_BookletChart.pdf.

RAINY DAY

USS North Carolina *#1 Battleship Way, Wilmington; 910-251-5797; battleshipnc.com*

It's not the kind of boating we usually recommend, but you can't beat exploring all nine (!) levels of this WWII battleship-turned-monument on a self-guided tour. (Your tent will never feel too small again after seeing where the sailors had to sleep.) Hours change seasonally and several ticket options are available; call or check website.

FOOD AND DRINK 🍺

Front Street Brewery *9 N. Front St., Wilmington; 910-251-1935; frontstreetbrewery.com*

Saddle up to the bar and order the $1.50 Mug of the Day. If you're lucky, it will be the El Hefe, a German-style unfiltered Hefeweizen with hints of banana and citrus—but consider yourself lucky to get any of their awesome brews at this price. Whiskey lovers will drool at the wall of whiskey.

Good Hops Brewing *811 Harper Ave., Carolina Beach; 706-713-1594; goodhopsbrewing.com*

A dog-friendly brewery, minutes from Carolina Beach State Park, with a side of disc golf? Yes, please! The beers at this low-key brewery go down easy, and a visit here is a great way to refresh and rehash before heading back to camp to make dinner.

Wake N Bake *1401 N. Lake Park Blvd., Carolina Beach; 910-707-0166; wakenbakedonuts.com*

Maybe the camp oatmeal just isn't getting you moving. Time to call in reinforcements . . . like Girl Scout cookie–inspired donuts and good coffee, served by staff who are just as happy to be there as you'll be.

Flaming Amy's Burrito Barn *1140-A N. Lake Park Blvd., Carolina Beach; 910-458-2563; flamingamys.com*

Why let Mexican food have all the burrito fun? Classic burrito offerings, along with ones boasting a Caribbean, Asian, or Greek flare. Not gimmicky, just good stuff.

GEAR AND RESUPPLY 🛒

Head left out of Carolina Beach State Park, and then turn left onto Dow Road for drugstores, beach shops, and a Food Lion; all are within 1.5 miles of the park entrance.

Great Outdoor Provision Company *3501 Oleander Dr., Wilmington; 910-343-1648; greatoutdoorprovisioncompany.com*

If it's outdoor gear and you need it, want it, or forgot it, they'll most likely have it.

Zeke's Island

ADDITIONAL RESOURCES

BIKING

Blueridgebicycleclub.org Members have access to more than 200 comprehensive road bike cue sheets across North Carolina.

Mtbproject.com Trail info, route suggestions, interactive maps with virtual tours, trail ratings, local contact information, and photos.

Mtbikewnc.com Guide to off-road bike trails in Western North Carolina; search for rides by location or difficulty.

Singletracks.com Off-road riding beta, including trail descriptions, directions, maps, route suggestions, and nearby lodging and trail reviews. Plus gear reviews, videos, and how-to information.

Sirbikesalot.com Growing database of off-road trails, with a focus on North Carolina. In-depth trail descriptions, including photos, videos, route info, history, and local group involvement.

Tarheeltrailblazers.com Up-to-date, locals-centric information (including trail closures) on North Carolina mountain bike trails.

Traillink.com Rails-to-Trails Conservancy site. Search greenway trails by state. Provides general information, parking and access points, and maps.

Trianglemtb.com Trail descriptions and closures, maps, user reviews, and current news on singletrack and doubletrack trails in the Triangle area.

CAMPING

The Best in Tent Camping: The Carolinas **by Johnny Molloy** A go-to resource for high-quality campgrounds for tent campers throughout North Carolina; includes site suggestions, campground maps, local recreation, and directions.

CLIMBING

Carolina Rocks: The Piedmont **by Erica Lineberry** Detailed guide to hiking in Central North Carolina, including Crowders Mountain routes. Routes clearly outlined on photographs.

Carolinaclimbers.org The Carolina Climbers Coalition exists to preserve and protect climbing areas in North Carolina. Site has general information on climbing throughout the Southeast, area closures, and other up-to-date climbing data.

Mountainproject.com General information on climbing areas worldwide, along with specific route descriptions, user comments, photos, and ratings.

Selected Climbs in North Carolina **by Yon Lambert and Harrison Shull** Thorough coverage of climbing areas, divided by region. Includes route data (detailed maps, level of difficulty, number of pitches) as well as access information, regular closures, registration requirements, best season for each area, nearby camping, and gear suggestions.

Summitpost.org Online climbing community with user-generated content. Climbing areas, routes with photographs and illustrations, topo maps, climbing news, natural history, and driving directions.

HIKING

100 Classic Hikes in North Carolina **by Joe Miller** Extensive selection of hikes throughout the state; especially helpful for families and planning coastal hikes.

Five-Star Trails: Asheville: Your Guide to the Area's Most Beautiful Hikes **by Jennifer Pharr Davis** Easy-to-use, easy-to-pack guide to both short and long hiking trails around Asheville.

Five-Star Trails: Charlotte: Your Guide to the Area's Most Beautiful Hikes **by Joshua Kinser** Detailed descriptions of hikes in Charlotte and surrounding areas, including McDowell Nature Center and Preserve and Crowders Mountain.

Five-Star Trails: Raleigh & Durham: Your Guide to the Area's Most Beautiful Hikes **by Joshua Kinser** Detailed descriptions of hikes in the Research Triangle area, including Eno River and William B. Umstead State Parks.

Hiking the Carolina Mountains **by Danny Bernstein** Includes more than 50 day hikes from 2–13 miles, trail maps, area history, and natural features. Good resource for longer day hikes.

Hiking North Carolina's National Forests: 50 Can't-Miss Trail Adventures in the Pisgah, Nantahala, Uwharrie, and Croatan National Forests **by Johnny Molloy** Thorough coverage of trails with detailed hike descriptions, maps, history, and relevant information on the state's national forests.

Hikingproject.com Trail information, including interactive maps, route options, elevation charts, photos, ratings, and local events.

Hikingthecarolinas.com Informal but comprehensive trail information for North Carolina and other Southeastern hiking destinations, presented by an enthusiastic trio of hikers.

Hikewnc.info Database of hikes in Western North Carolina; searchable by difficulty and trail features. Links to useful maps.

Linvillegorge.net User group with lots of up-to-date trail information, GPS tracks, maps, and other useful information on the Linville Gorge area. Must create a free account to access map information.

Ncmst.org Friends of the Mountains-to-Sea Trail site with trail updates, an interactive map, comprehensive trail guide, and day hike recommendations.

Neusioktrail.org Regularly updated information on the Neusiok Trail, curated by an avid hiker.

PADDLING

Americanwhitewater.org Site of American Whitewater, a nonprofit organization devoted to river stewardship. General river information, user-reported flow data, rapid descriptions, and trip reports.

Boatingbeta.com Asheville-area flatwater and whitewater information, including release schedules.

***Carolina Whitewater: A Paddler's Guide to the Western Carolinas* by David and Bob Benner** Detailed run information on Western North Carolina rivers, including the French Broad, Green, and Nantahala Rivers.

***Guide to Sea Kayaking in North Carolina: The Best Day Trips and Tours from Currituck to Cape Fear* by Pam Malec** Guide to dozens of paddling trips along the North Carolina coast, with put-in and takeout locations, trip descriptions, local wildlife, camping information, and restaurant recommendations.

Paddling.com Most helpful for its river trip reports and launch site maps. Also has gear reviews, general information on kayak, canoe, and SUP paddling, and a community message board.

***Paddling Eastern North Carolina* by Paul G. Ferguson** Comprehensive guide to whitewater and flatwater opportunities from the Yadkin-Pee Dee Basin to the coast. Includes put-in and takeout information, section descriptions, difficulty and scenery ratings, and gauge locations.

Raleighnc.gov Clear and concise information on public boat access points on the Neuse River; linked to map data.

WILDLIFE

***Living Beaches of Georgia and the Carolinas: A Beachcomber's Guide* by Blair and Dawn Witherington** Full-color resource, helpful for coastal flora and fauna identification.

Ncbirdingtrail.org The Sites tab is useful for finding general trail and habitat information throughout North Carolina, and gives detailed lists of the birds found at each site and the best time of year to spot them.

Ncwildlife.org Information on North Carolina's species and habitats; also includes boating beta and tips on bird-watching and nature photography.

GENERAL INFORMATION

Ashevillenow.com Information on camping, paddling, hiking, and climbing in Asheville and surrounding areas.

Blue Ridge Outdoors and blueridgeoutdoors.com Free monthly magazine; good-quality, comprehensive coverage of outdoor life throughout the Blue Ridge. Trip itineraries, gear reviews, current trends, environmental issues, music, and more.

Getgoingnc.com Launched by guidebook author Joe Miller with the support of Blue Cross Blue Shield of North Carolina, this site lists many ways to be active in the great outdoors. Helpful resource for finding outdoor activities of all kinds throughout North Carolina.

Landtrustcnc.org Useful resource about land trust-protected areas in North Carolina, especially the Uwharrie National Forest.

Lnt.org The Leave No Trace Center for Outdoor Ethics promotes sustainable use of the outdoors, and their site provides numerous easy-to-follow guidelines for whenever you play outside.

Nccoastalreserve.net Website of the N.C. Coastal Reserve and National Estuarine Research Reserve; offers helpful information on Masonboro Island Reserve.

NCwaterfalls.com Lists waterfalls in Western North Carolina by area, and includes driving directions.

Our State and ourstate.com North Carolina-based magazine with extensive travel information and current events.

Romanticasheville.com Guide to Asheville and surrounding areas; hike recommendations, events, and lodging information.

Rootsrated.com Outdoor beta presented through articles and stories; covers a broad variety of activities from disc golf to fat-tire biking.

***Uwharrie Lakes Region Trail Guide: Hiking and Biking in North Carolina's Uwharrie Mountains* by Don Childrey** Incredibly thorough descriptions of Uwharrie's bike, hike, OHV, and equestrian trails. Detailed maps, elevation profiles, GPS coordinates, and hike suggestions.

Visitnc.com If it's in North Carolina, it's probably on this site. Good for contact information and day trip ideas.

INDEX

American Hiking Society

Protect the places you love to explore.

Become a member today before you hit the trails in North Carolina and take $5 off using the code NCWILD.

AmericanHiking.org/join

American Hiking Society is a 501(c)3 non-profit organization which believes that hiking provides a pathway to health, mental well-being, and appreciation of natural spaces.

ACKNOWLEDGMENTS

Writing this book was a feat of love, sweat (so much sweat), and beers.

We would like to thank everyone who supports outdoor recreation in North Carolina through his or her work, volunteerism, advocacy, or financial support.

Thank you to Andy Zivinski and Diane Cutler for putting up with us every time we pop into their bike shop and don't buy any bikes. Thank you to Chad Clark for getting us zipping through the treetops of Asheville. Thanks to Chris Cagle for sharing the best paddling spots in Uwharrie. Thanks to David Hoskins for letting us barge into his outfitters in the off-season and still giving us all the Danbury information and beer-themed swag we could ever want. Thanks to Daniel Sapp and Shaunna Richard for sharing their Pisgah-area expertise with us on a beautiful Saturday morning. Thanks to Steven Houser for giving us the lowdown on Saluda when we showed up to his campground at the last minute one evening. Thanks to Ryan Kaufman and Jessica Whitmire for letting us pick their brains about paddling on the French Broad River. Thank you to Pam Pearson for sharing her paddling expertise and adding lots of other state parks to our to-do list. Thank you to Tyler Jackson for telling us about all the amazing paddling opportunities in the Outer Banks. Thanks to Aaron West for patiently teaching us what we needed to know about surfing and vegan food on Cape Hatteras. Thank you to Natasha Teasley for giving us the full scoop on paddling around Raleigh.

A big thank-you to Tim Jackson for his fervent support of this project, for answering never-ending questions, and for introducing us to really amazing Mexican food in Asheville. Thank you to the AdventureKEEN team for all they did in getting this book concept off the ground, and to Holly Cross and Adam Rosen for their advice, insights, and positive feedback. Thank you to Tyler Boeing and Brekken Casey for one of our best days of paddling ever on the Green River. Thanks to Todd Horsley for always responding to our cries of help whenever we needed suggestions. Thank you to Adam Fancher for being our Charlotte guru and for his nonstop enthusiasm. Thank you to our parents for nurturing our love of the great outdoors, albeit in their own ways. And a huge thank you to our friends and family for their nonstop love, support, and excitement for this book.

ABOUT THE AUTHORS

Jessie Johnson started her life of adventure by tromping through the woods behind her childhood home in North Carolina. Camping, hiking, backpacking, paddling, climbing, biking, surfing—if you can do it outside, she's in! With years of practice, she and Matt perfected the ultimate weekend adventure. Matt would pick her up at work every Friday, bikes and burritos ready to go. She's been a children's librarian, outdoor educator, Girl Scout troop leader, and sea turtle patrol volunteer. Most recently, Jessie has been lucky enough to turn her weekend adventures into every day adventures as a Subaru/Leave No Trace traveling trainer and is crisscrossing the western United States with Matt, teaching people how to play outside in sustainable ways. She now gets to camp 250 nights a year!

Matt Schneider began adventuring at a young age: first while being carried in a backpack, and then while trying to catch up to his parents across trails, down rivers, and up mountains. After earning his Eagle Scout, Matt became a camp counselor, outdoor trip leader, philosophy professor, and challenge course manager (in that order). He has paddled, pedaled, hiked, climbed, surfed, and caved on three continents and in 11 countries and 32 states over the years. When not competing in off-road triathlons or researching his next book, he can be found living on the road with Jessie, teaching outdoor ethics as a Subaru/Leave No Trace traveling trainer.

CPSIA information can be obtained
at www.ICGtesting.com
Printed in the USA
BVHW09*1712091018
529537BV00004B/18/P

9 781634 042277